WHAT SMALL GROUP LEADERS AND MEMBERS ARE SAYING ABOUT EXPERIENCING CHRIST TOGETHER

My group was formed four years ago of very new believers. EXPERIENCING CHRIST TOGETHER has helped form bonds, and we have fallen in love with Christ. We have had many trials, but we have learned to lean on the body of Christ to carry us through the difficult times. I know our lives are richer than ever.

—Leader

The EXPERIENCING CHRIST TOGETHER series has motivated me more than any other Bible study that I have ever been to. This Bible study gets to the heart of the matter—my character in Christ—and that has created action on my part.

—Leader

I love the fact that Jesus' life shows us how to live.

—Member

This series is an "awakening." Jesus has become a very personal friend.

—Leader

This series is definitely a must-do as the foundation for a healthy, maturing small group!

—Leader

EXPERIENCING CHRIST TOGETHER is a safe place to learn about the living Jesus and how he wants to lead us and love us.

—Member

EXPERIENCING CHRIST TOGETHER ties the heart and the mind together. The Bible knowledge grows the mind and the life application grows the heart and transforms the soul.

—Member

Other Studies in the EXPERIENCING CHRIST TOGETHER Series

Beginning in Christ Together (Life of Jesus)

Growing in Christ Together (Discipleship)

Serving Like Christ Together (Ministry)

Sharing Christ Together (Evangelism)

Surrendering to Christ Together (Worship)

Studies in the DOING LIFE TOGETHER Series

Beginning Life Together (God's Purpose for Your Life)

Connecting with God's Family (Fellowship)

Growing to Be Like Christ (Discipleship)

Developing Your SHAPE to Serve Others (Ministry)

Sharing Your Life Mission Every Day (Evangelism)

Surrendering Your Life to God's Pleasure (Worship)

CONNECTING IN CHRIST TOGETHER

six sessions on
Fellowship

written by
BRETT and **DEE EASTMAN**
TODD and **DENISE WENDORFF**
KAREN LEE-THORP

GRAND RAPIDS, MICHIGAN 49530 USA

ZONDERVAN™

Connecting in Christ Together
Copyright © 2005 by Brett and Deanna Eastman, Todd and Denise Wendorff,
and Karen Lee-Thorp

Requests for information should be addressed to:

Zondervan, *Grand Rapids, Michigan 49530*

ISBN 0-310-24981-3

Interior icons by Tom Clark

Interior design by Beth Shagene & Michelle Espinoza

Printed in the United States of America

05 06 07 08 09 10 11 /❖ DCI/ 10 9 8 7 6 5 4 3 2

CONTENTS

EXPERIENCING CHRIST TOGETHER

EXPERIENCING CHRIST TOGETHER: LIVING WITH PURPOSE IN COMMUNITY will take you face to face with Jesus himself. In addition to being the Son of God and Savior of the world, Jesus holds the greatest wisdom and understands the purposes for which God formed you. He knows what it takes to build authentic relationships, to know God more intensely, to grow spiritually, and ultimately to make a difference in the world. EXPERIENCING CHRIST TOGETHER offers you a chance to do what Jesus' first followers did: spend time with him, listen to what he said, watch what he did, and pattern your life after his.

Jesus lived every moment following God's purpose for his life. In this study you will experience firsthand how he did this and how you can do it too. Yet if you're anything like us, knowing what God wants for you is one thing, but doing it is something else. That's why you'll follow Jesus' plan of doing life not alone but together. As you follow in his footsteps, you'll find his pathway more exciting than anything you've imagined.

Book 1 of this series (*Beginning in Christ Together*) explores the person of Jesus Christ. Each of the subsequent five studies looks through Jesus' eyes at one of God's five biblical purposes for his people (fellowship, discipleship, service, evangelism, and worship). For example, *Connecting in Christ Together* deals with fellowship. Book 1 is about grace: what Christ has done for us. The other books are about how we live in response to grace.

Even if you've done another LIFE TOGETHER study, you'll be amazed at how Jesus can take you to places of faith you've never been before. The joy of life in him is far beyond a life you could design on your own. If you do all six study guides in this series, you'll spend one astonishing year with Jesus Christ.

The Power of Love

The Christian movement of the first few centuries AD won hearts from Spain to Syria despite intense persecution and competition from other religions. One important attraction was love. Thousands of people embraced Christian faith partly because Christians loved one another and their non-Christian neighbors in practical ways that astounded the ancient world. The fourth-century emperor Julian, for instance, regarded Christians as "atheists" because they rejected the traditional Roman gods, and he was frustrated that so many pagans were converting. Julian complained, "Why do we not observe that it is their benevolence to strangers, their care for the graves of the dead, and the pretended holiness of their lives that have done most to increase atheism [Christianity]? . . .[I]t is disgraceful," he went on, "that when no Jew ever has to beg, and the impious Galileans [Christians] support not only their poor but ours as well, all men see that our people lack aid from us."[1]

Today, love is not always the first thing that springs to mind when unbelievers think about Christians. But it should be. It can be. By our choices, we can make it so.

Our mandate from Jesus is simple: "Love one another as I have loved you." We are to grasp the breadth and depth of his love for us, and then treat others in the same way. This study aims to help you do those two things—come to grips with Jesus' love for you and explore how you can follow his example. Your small group will be a place to practice giving and receiving Jesus' kind of love.

What Christians call "fellowship" is one of God's core dreams for his people. It's simply love, passionate and practical. If you need more of that in your life and your group, let Jesus show you how.

Outline of Each Session

Most people want to live healthy, balanced spiritual lives, but few achieve this alone. And most small groups struggle to balance all of God's purposes in their meetings. Groups tend to overemphasize one of the five purposes, perhaps fellowship or discipleship. Rarely is there a healthy balance that includes evangelism, ministry, and worship. That's why we've included all of these elements in this study so you can live a healthy, balanced spiritual life over time.

A typical group session will include the following:

 CONNECTING WITH GOD'S FAMILY (FELLOWSHIP). The foundation for spiritual growth is an intimate connection with God and his family. A few people who really know you and who earn your trust

[1]*Epistula ad SPQ Atheniarum* 84a. Bidez-Cumont-*Epistula ad SPQ Atheniarum* 22 Wright (Loeb Classical Library Edition) 429D–430D, quoted in John G. Gager, "Religion and Social Class in the Early Roman Empire," Stephen Benko and John J. O'Rourke, eds., *The Catacombs and the Colosseum* (Valley Forge, Pa.: Judson Press, 1971), 113.

provide a place to experience the life Jesus invites you to live. This section of each session typically offers you two options. You can get to know your whole group by using the icebreaker question (always question 1), or you can check in with one or two group members—your spiritual partner(s)—for a deeper connection and encouragement in your spiritual journey.

DVD TEACHING SEGMENT. A DVD companion to this study guide is available. For each study session, a teacher discusses the topic, ordinary Christians talk about the personal experience of the topic, a scholar gives background on the Bible passage, and a leadership coach gives tips to the group leader. The DVD contains worship helps and other features as well. If you are using the DVD, you will view the teaching segment after your Connecting discussion and before your Bible study (the Growing section). At the end of each session in this study guide you will find space for your notes on the teaching segment. To view a sample of the DVD, log on to www.lifetogether.com/ExperiencingChristTogether.

 GROWING TO BE LIKE CHRIST (DISCIPLESHIP). Here is where you come face to face with Christ. In a core Bible passage you'll see Jesus in action, teaching or demonstrating some aspect of how he wants you to live. The focus won't be on accumulating information but on how Jesus' words and actions relate to what you say and do. We want to help you apply the Scriptures practically, creatively, and from your heart as well as your head. At the end of the day, allowing the timeless truths from God's word to transform our lives in Christ is our greatest aim.

FOR DEEPER STUDY. If you want to dig deeper into more Bible passages about the topic at hand, we've provided additional passages and questions. Your group may choose to do study homework ahead of each meeting in order to cover more biblical material. Or you as an individual may choose to study the For Deeper Study passages on your own. If you prefer not to do study homework, the Growing section will provide you with plenty to discuss within the group. These options allow individuals or the whole group to go deeper in their study, while still accommodating those who can't do homework or are new to your group.

You can record your discoveries on the Reflections page at the end of each session. We encourage you to read some of your insights to a friend (spiritual partner) for accountability and support. Spiritual partners may check in each week over the phone, through email, or at the beginning of the group meeting.

 DEVELOPING YOUR GIFTS TO SERVE OTHERS (MINISTRY). Jesus trained his disciples to discover and develop their gifts to serve others. God has designed you uniquely to serve him in a way no other person can. This section will help you discover and use your God-given design. It will also encourage your group to discover your unique design as a community. In two sessions in this study, you'll put into practice what you've learned in the Bible study by taking a step to serve others. These simple steps will take your group on a faith journey that could change your lives forever.

 SHARING YOUR LIFE MISSION EVERY DAY (EVANGELISM). Many people skip over this aspect of the Christian life because it's scary, relationally awkward, or simply too much work for their busy schedules. But Jesus wanted all of his disciples to help outsiders connect with him, to know him personally. This doesn't mean preaching on street corners. It could mean welcoming a few newcomers into your group, hosting a short-term group in your home, participating in a cross-cultural missions project, or walking through this study with a friend. In four sessions of this study, you'll have an opportunity to take a small step in this area. These steps will take you beyond Bible study to Bible living.

 SURRENDERING YOUR LIFE FOR GOD'S PLEASURE (WORSHIP). God is most pleased by a heart that is fully his. Each group session will give you a chance to surrender your heart to God in prayer and worship. You may read a psalm together, share a page in your journal, or use one of the songs on the DVD to open or close your meeting. (Additional music is available on the LIFE TOGETHER Worship DVD/CD series, produced by Maranatha!) If you've never prayed aloud in a group before, no one will put pressure on you. Instead, you'll experience the support of others who are praying for you. This time will knit your hearts in community and help you surrender all your hurts and dreams into the hands of the One who knows you best.

STUDY NOTES. This section provides background notes on the Bible passage(s) you examine in the Growing section. You may want to refer to these notes during your group meeting or as a reference for those doing additional study.

REFLECTIONS. At the end of each session is a blank page on which you can write your insights from your personal time with God. Whether you do deeper Bible study, read through the Gospels, meditate on a few verses, or simply write out your prayers, you'll benefit from writing down what you discover. You may want to pick up a blank journal or notepad after you fill in these pages.

AS I HAVE LOVED YOU

Robin was born with defective kidneys. He had two kidney transplants as a child and a third as a young adult. In his late thirties he needed a fourth transplant. Unfortunately, the waiting list for a kidney from a deceased donor was six years. Realistically, then, someone who loved him needed to give him a kidney.

Six of Robin's friends each offered a kidney. The doctors picked their top three choices among the six, and those three worked out among themselves that his friend Amy would be the one to save Robin's life.

Loving one another often costs time. Effort. Even money. But what can one say about friends who are willing to give the organs of their bodies for one another? Your friendships may never need to go that far, but as you consider Jesus' words about love in this session, ask yourself how far you would go for a friend.

CONNECTING WITH GOD'S FAMILY   20 min.

There's something about sharing personal stories that deepens your connections with each other. That's why each session in this guide begins with an opportunity to hear one another's experiences.

1. Take sixty seconds to respond briefly to one of the following:

   ☐ Think of a time when someone loved you. It could be a current experience or one long past. What did that person do that was loving?
   ☐ Describe a time when you experienced God's love.

2. Whether your group is brand new or ongoing, it's always important to reflect on and review your values together. On pages 80–81 is a sample agreement with the values we've found most useful in sustaining healthy, balanced groups. We recommend that you choose one or two values—ones you haven't previously focused on or have room to grow in—to emphasize

during this study. Choose ones that will take your group to the next stage of intimacy and spiritual health.

☐ **For new groups:** You may want to focus on building a safe environment. If a group isn't a safe place for people to share themselves, nothing else happens.

☐ **For existing groups:** We recommend that you rotate host homes on a regular basis and let the hosts lead the meeting. We've come to realize that healthy groups rotate leadership. This helps to develop every member's ability to shepherd a few people in a safe environment. Even Jesus gave others the opportunity to serve alongside him (Mark 6:30–44). Session 3 will explain how to set up a rotating schedule.

 GROWING TO BE LIKE CHRIST   40 min.

John 15:9–17 is part of the final teaching Jesus gave his followers—his disciples or students—right before he was crucified. Everything he had trained them to be culminated here. Love was an essential mark of Jesus' students. In fact, it was *the* sign by which outsiders would recognize those who belonged to Jesus (John 13:35). It was also the glue that bonded them first to him and then to one another. Without a deep commitment to love each other, they would never have changed the world as they did.

Love is the ultimate test of whether you have Christ in you or not. Jesus' kind of love is difficult—it's nearly impossible to sustain if his life isn't welling up from within you. Jesus' kind of love puts your desires on the back burner and focuses on another person. It sets aside personal gain. It gives; it builds up the other. This is not the "love" sentimentalized in greeting cards and pop songs. It's something much more costly.

3. Read John 15:9–17. Exactly what does Jesus tell his followers to do in this passage? Note especially the instructions he repeats more than once.

4. Why does he repeat himself, even to these disciples who know him well?

5. Jesus defines the word "love" by pointing at himself—paying the ultimate price (verses 12–13). How would you describe this kind of love (for example, affectionate, romantic, etc.)?

6. What is the connection between loving others and remaining (abiding, dwelling) in Christ's love for us?

7. The quality of our love for others reflects the degree to which we are gripped by Jesus' love for us. What do you think helps a person become more motivated by Christ's love?

8. Turn to 1 John 3:16–18. What is one way we can lay down our lives for each other?

9. What other ways of laying down our lives for each other can you think of?

10. Has anyone other than Jesus ever laid down his or her life for you? If so, briefly describe what that person did.

11. Whom in your life is God reminding you to love?

12. The more you "remain" or "abide" in Jesus' love for you, the more you'll love others. Likewise, the more you love others, the more you'll abide in his love (John 15:9–10). Abiding in his love is a moment-by-moment awareness that Jesus is present, now, loving you.

    Immersing yourself in the Bible and prayer will help you cultivate that moment-by-moment awareness. Here are several options for doing this for the next six weeks. Which one will you commit to pursue?

    ☐ *Prayer.* Identify someone whom you have trouble loving. Commit to praying for that person throughout this study, both with your group and on your own. Ask God to show you his attitude toward the person. Ask him to help you to love the person the way Jesus would. You may find it helpful to write your prayers on the Reflections page included at the end of every session.

    ☐ *Gospel Reading.* Read through the gospel of Luke. On pages 93–94 is a reading plan. As you read, we recommend that you jot down your thoughts on the Reflections page or in a journal.

    ☐ *Meditation.* If you've read Luke before, try meditation as a way of internalizing God's Word more deeply. Copy a portion of each week's Bible study passage onto a card, and tape it somewhere in your line of sight, such as your car's dashboard or the kitchen table. Think about it when you sit at red lights, or while you're eating a meal. What is God saying to you, here and now, through these words? Several alternative passages for meditation are suggested on the Reflections page in each session. You may use that page to write your responses to your meditation verses.

On pages 24–25 is a Personal Health Plan, a chart for keeping track of your spiritual progress. In the box that says, "WHAT is your next step for growth?" write the step you chose in question 12.

FOR DEEPER STUDY

Read 1 John 4:7–21. Why does John think love is so essential for us to practice?

Look at Jesus' example of love for his disciples in John 13:1–17, 34–35. Why is love (rather than something else) the mark of a true disciple? What would it look like to wash each other's feet in today's society?

Read Isaiah 53:1–9 and Philippians 2:1–11. What did Jesus' kind of love involve? What in these passages motivates you to love? How are we supposed to follow Jesus' example?

Read Romans 5:6–8. Here Paul emphasizes that Jesus' love was unusual. How, then, can we take his example as one we should follow?

13. Many groups find they're having such a good time with each other that they don't want to open their circle to new people. Why "start over" with a stranger when you already have enough friends? But when you were a stranger to God, and he already had all the love he needed, he widened the circle of his love to include you. Opening your group from time to time is a way of laying down your group life for others.

The following "Circles of Life" diagram will help you think of the various people you come in contact with on a regular basis. Prayerfully write down at least three or four names in the circles.

CIRCLES OF LIFE

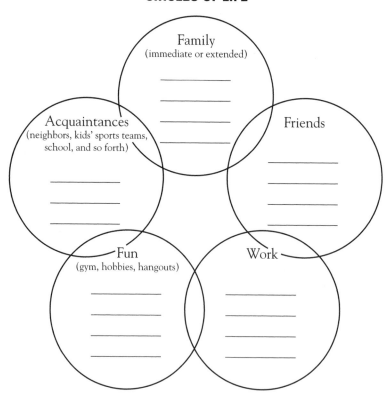

Which of these people can you invite to join this group for your next meeting? Ask the group to pray for you in this, as well as for the people you're inviting.

SURRENDERING YOUR LIFE FOR GOD'S PLEASURE   15–30 min.

14. How can the group pray for you this week? Write people's prayer requests in the Prayer and Praise Report on page 21.

15. Listen to people's prayer requests. How can you help out someone in your group?

16. When we truly see Jesus as the One who laid down his life for us, worship naturally follows. Take some time to respond to Jesus' love for you.

   Read Psalm 136 aloud together. This psalm has a repeated refrain that makes it ideal for reading aloud. Have one person read the first line of each verse ("Give thanks to the LORD, for he is good"), and let the whole group read the refrain ("His love endures forever"). When you finish the last verse, allow some silence in which group members can add their own one-sentence thanksgivings (for example, "He offered his life for our sins" or "He is healing John's sister"). After each thanksgiving, the group can respond with the same refrain ("His love endures forever").

   You can use this same sentence-and-response structure to pray for the requests you listed in question 14, or you can have some open time for people to pray as they wish.

STUDY NOTES

Love[d] (John 15:9, 10, 12, 13, 17). The Greek verb "to love" (*agapaō*) and the related noun (*agapē*) that Jesus uses in this passage weren't the most commonly used words for love in Classical Greek. But when the Jews translated the Old Testament into Greek, they chose this word group to render Hebrew words that described God's love for humans. Thus, to define what Jesus meant by *agapē*, scholars don't turn to Greek dictionaries. They look at the behavior of God in the Old Testament and the behavior of Christ in the New Testament. "Love" means "what God does."[2]

---

[2]W. Günther and H. G. Link, "Love," *The New International Dictionary of New Testament Theology*, CD-ROM version (Grand Rapids: Zondervan, 1999).

To love someone is to will (desire, choose, intend, pursue) good for him. It involves good intention and action. It cost God what he valued most (his Son's life) to love us. So we can expect love to be costly in time, effort, and even suffering.

Remain in my love (John 15:9). Jesus uses the word "remain" (or "abide") seven times in John 15:1–10. The word means to last a long time, to endure, or to stay. Christ's love endures. It withstands the test of time and trouble. To remain in him is to stay with him, go where he goes, maintain constant awareness of his presence and his love—and thereby to love as he loves.

Material possessions (1 John 3:17). John lived in a society where most people had just enough food, clothing, and shelter to survive, and no money saved for emergencies. In such a society, people knew they could at any time become dependent upon others for survival. The few affluent people in a given church would have been far outnumbered by the many who were barely getting by. John was asking a lot for these people to lay down their lives (and possessions) for their fellow Christians.

In our society, it is possible to go to a Christian group and not rub shoulders with people who are surviving paycheck to paycheck. Affluence breeds independence and a desire for self-sufficiency. If a person is doing pretty well financially, he may not want help from a fellow Christian, and he may not want to help others either. He's self-sufficient; why shouldn't they be?

Time is a commodity in our culture too. A person may want never to need someone else's time, and she may not want others to need her time either. Again, she places a high value on independence and self-sufficiency. For such a person, following Jesus will require a new way of thinking.

PRAYER AND PRAISE REPORT

Briefly share your prayer requests with the large group, making notations below. Then gather in smaller groups of two to four to pray for each other.

Date: _____

Prayer Requests

_____

_____

_____

_____

_____

_____

_____

_____

_____

Praise Report

_____

_____

_____

_____

_____

_____

_____

_____

_____

_____

REFLECTIONS

Use this page to write out your prayers, your thoughts about your daily Bible reading, or your meditations on a verse from the passage you have already studied. Below are some suggested verses for meditation. The Bible Reading Plan is on pages 93–94.

For Meditation: John 15:9–10 or 15:12–13

For Gospel Reading:

- What do I *learn* from the life of Christ (his identity, personality, priorities)?

- How does he want me to *live* differently?

_____

_____

_____

_____

_____

_____

_____

_____

_____

_____

_____

_____

_____

_____

_____

_____

_____

_____

DVD NOTES

If you are watching the accompanying *Connecting in Christ Together* DVD, write down what you sense God is saying to you through the speaker. (If you'd like to hear a sample of the DVD teaching segment, go to www.life-together.com/ExperiencingChristTogether.)

PERSONAL HEALTH PLAN

This worksheet could become your single most important feature in this study. On it you can record your personal priorities before the Father. It will help you live a healthy spiritual life, balancing all five of God's purposes.

PURPOSE	PLAN
CONNECT	WHO are you connecting with spiritually?
GROW	WHAT is your next step for growth?
DEVELOP	WHERE are you serving?
SHARE	WHEN are you shepherding another in Christ?
SURRENDER	HOW are you surrendering your heart?

If you have more than one partner, another Personal Health Plan can be found in the Appendix or downloaded in a larger format at www.lifeto-gether.com/healthplan. A Sample Health Plan is also in the Appendix.

DATE	MY PROGRESS	PARTNER'S PROGRESS

SHOWING UP

Five years ago, Bennie's wife, Margaret, was diagnosed with lung cancer. They were stunned. They and their loved ones trusted God for a miracle, and Margaret's first surgery was a great success. But eighteen months later, the doctors said the cancer had spread to her bones. She needed intensive chemotherapy and radiation.

Bennie and Margaret had never been in a small group. But soon after this second diagnosis, some friends invited them to join their group. Throughout Margaret's treatment, the group not only prayed diligently but made many sacrifices to help her and her husband. When money was tight, group members sometimes gave money. When Margaret needed a ride to an appointment, group members volunteered. They helped with meals. During a hot summer, they gave Margaret and Bennie an air conditioner. They took shifts caring for Margaret at home in order to give Bennie some time off. They cleaned up after Margaret when she was bedridden and held group meetings in her bedroom when she was too weak to travel. Bennie never had to ask for any of this—people simply anticipated the couple's need and responded.

Margaret is with God now. Bennie looks forward to the reunion he, Margaret, and their group will have in heaven, when Margaret will be able to thank each person for so many generous acts. In this session you'll think about what it might mean for you to care for one another generously.

CONNECTING WITH GOD'S FAMILY   10 min.

As people are gathering, play a song from a worship CD. When the song ends, pray briefly for God's presence in your time together. Then get started by responding briefly to question 1.

1. Have you ever suffered a significant loss (for example, a loved one's serious illness or death, your own serious illness, a job loss, or a divorce)? What did people do for you or your family in that situation? (Please limit your response to one minute so there's time for everyone to share.)

GROWING TO BE LIKE CHRIST 30 min.

Death exposes us to the core. When someone close to us dies, our response reveals how strong our connections are to God, to our families, and to our communities. Death can move us to withdraw or to connect more deeply. It can cause us to trust or mistrust God. When someone we know loses a loved one, our response to him or her also reveals much about us.

As with us, the impending death of Jesus' close friend Lazarus revealed Jesus' character and priorities. His ministry had put him so at odds with his country's leaders that he was liable to be arrested if he went near the capital city. But Lazarus was dying just a few miles outside the capital. What would Jesus do, his disciples wondered, when he heard of his friend's illness?

> **2.** Read John 11. What signs do you see in verses 1–16 that it's risky for Jesus to go to Lazarus? (The study notes on verses 1 and 7 may help here.)

> **3.** How would you describe the way Jesus and Martha relate to each other in verses 17–27?

> **4.** How does Mary relate to Jesus in verses 28–37?

> How does he respond to her?

5. What does Jesus do for his friend that only he can do (verses 38–44)?

What does Jesus have others do?

6. When our friends are suffering, we can't do everything Jesus does for Lazarus. Yet what hope does this story give us that we can offer to others? (See, for example, verses 25–26.)

7. What price does Jesus pay for intervening on his friends' behalf (verses 45–53)?

8. What impression of Jesus as a person do you get from this story?

9. What can we learn from this story about how to respond to people in pain?

FOR DEEPER STUDY

On the topic of sacrificial care for a friend, see the life priorities Jesus described in Matthew 25:31–46. Why did Jesus see these priorities as so essential?

See also how Timothy and Epaphroditus cared for Paul in prison (Philippians 2:19–30). Why did Epaphroditus risk his health for Paul's sake? What are you willing to do for your friends, and where do you draw the line?

DEVELOPING YOUR GIFTS TO SERVE OTHERS   10 min.

10. Pair up with someone in your group. (We suggest that men partner with men and women with women.) This person will be your "spiritual partner" during this study.

   Back in question 12 of session 1, you set a goal for personal time with God. Your partner's job is to encourage you as you pursue that goal. Following through on a resolution is tough when you're on your own, but we've found it makes all the difference to have a partner cheering us on. This person doesn't have to be your best friend, just someone who will be faithful to check in with you.

   Turn to your Personal Health Plan on pages 24–25. In the box that says, "WHO are you connecting with spiritually?" write your partner's name.

   Tell your partner what you wrote under "WHAT is your next step for growth?" When you check in with your partner each week during this study, your health plan will provide a place to record your own progress and your partner's progress in fulfilling your goals.

It's okay to have two partners. If you have two, an additional health plan is on pages 88–89 in the Appendix. Also, on pages 90–91 you'll find a completed health plan filled in as an example.

SURRENDERING YOUR LIFE FOR GOD'S PLEASURE 15–30 min.

11. How can the group pray for you this week? Perhaps the story of Lazarus brings to mind needs in your own life.

12. As you finish praying for the needs shared in question 11, play a worship song or offer thanks to Christ for caring for you as he cared for Mary, Martha, and Lazarus.

   During the week, continue to support each other with your prayers. And consider checking in with someone who mentioned a significant need. Even a quick call or email can make a big difference.

STUDY NOTES

Jesus demonstrated what it looks like to love sacrificially. Lazarus, Martha, and Mary were some of Jesus' best friends (see Luke 10:38–42). So his disciples weren't surprised that he wanted to go to them when Lazarus got sick. But this visit wasn't just an inconvenience in a busy schedule. It placed Jesus' life at risk. His disciples were shocked that he was willing to take love for his friends so far. His actions called into question their limited ideas of love.

Bethany (John 11:1). Less than two miles from Jerusalem, which was the capital of Judea.

Back to Judea (11:7). Conflict between Jesus and the authorities in Jerusalem was so intense that the authorities tried to provoke a mob to kill him (John 10:31–39). After that, Jesus retreated across the Jordan River, outside their jurisdiction (10:40). Traveling to Bethany would put him back in his enemies' territory. This decision to go to Bethany led directly to the authorities' decision to crucify him (11:45–57; 12:1, 12–28).

I am the resurrection (11:25). Different Jewish groups had different expectations about the afterlife. Some thought life ended at death. Some shared the Greek view that souls were immortal and would be liberated when they could shed their bodies. Jesus sided with those Jews who believed God was going to resurrect his people whole—soul and body—when God's kingdom came in its fullness. And Jesus went further: he claimed that the resurrection was possible only through him.

Deeply moved in spirit and troubled (11:33). The Greek words here don't mean sadness over the loss of Lazarus; Jesus knew Lazarus would be alive again in minutes. Rather, the words refer to anger. Jesus was profoundly angry at death, an enemy he was sworn to destroy. He was also profoundly grieved that not even Mary and Martha, let alone their friends, believed he had the power to overcome death (see 11:23–27, 32, 37, 40).

PRAYER AND PRAISE REPORT

Briefly share your prayer requests with the large group, making notations below. Then gather in smaller groups of two to four to pray for each other.

Date: _____

Prayer Requests

_____

_____

_____

_____

_____

_____

_____

_____

_____

_____

Praise Report

_____

_____

_____

_____

_____

_____

_____

_____

_____

_____

_____

_____

REFLECTIONS

Use this page to write out your prayers, your thoughts about your daily Bible reading, or your meditations on a verse from the passage you have already studied. Below are some suggested verses for meditation. The Bible Reading Plan is on pages 93–94.

For Meditation: John 11:25–27 or 11:33–44

For Gospel Reading:

- What do I *learn* from the life of Christ (his identity, personality, priorities)?

- How does he want me to *live* differently?

DVD NOTES

If you are watching the accompanying *Connecting in Christ Together* DVD, write down what you sense God is saying to you through the speaker. (If you'd like to hear a sample of the DVD teaching segment, go to www.life-together.com/ExperiencingChristTogether.)

LOVING FLAWED PEOPLE

When Allen first met Steve, they were in high school gym class together. Steve was quiet and insecure, with few friends. Then Allen began to include Steve in his social life. At first their mutual love for partying drew them together. But as Allen started to grow spiritually, he lost interest in drinking and wild parties. In college, they drifted apart.

When Allen reconnected with Steve after college, Steve's life was a mess. He was drinking heavily and was addicted to sexually graphic literature. Allen stepped in to help. With few resources of his own and a new wife to attend to, Allen drove Steve out of state to a rehab center. Months passed and Steve continued to struggle with sin, but slowly Allen got through to him. He helped Steve establish a fully committed relationship with Christ and stuck with him through years of ups and downs. Steve often called Allen when desperate to return to his old life. Patiently, Allen continued to give his friend time and energy.

Today Steve is free from his addictive behaviors and growing stronger in Christ. Allen's commitment to love Steve, despite his persistent sin, has been worth the effort.

CONNECTING WITH GOD'S FAMILY   10 min.

This session is about loving people with persistent sin in their lives. You may begin with a chance for the whole group to connect (question 1) or with a chance for spiritual partners to check in one-on-one (question 2).

1. On a scale of one to ten, how has your week been? Take one sentence or less (be sensitive to others' time) to explain why.

10	5	1
heaven	earth	lower than low

2. Sit with your spiritual partner(s). If your partner is absent or if you are new to the group, join with another pair or with someone who is also partnerless.

Turn to your Personal Health Plan (pages 24–25). Share with your partner(s) how your time with God went this week. What is one thing you discovered, perhaps something you wrote in your journal? Or, what obstacles hindered you from following through? Also make a note about your partner's progress and how you can pray for him or her.

GROWING TO BE LIKE CHRIST   30–40 min.

A common instruction in Christian circles is "Hate the sin but love the sinner." This is easier said than done. It's difficult to treat someone with robust and compassionate love while hating something he or she habitually does. More often we tepidly tolerate someone whose behavior repels us, or we ignore the harmful behavior of someone we love.

We may be coolly civil to our immoral neighbor, but is that what Jesus would call love? And what about ignoring a Christian friend's compulsive shopping or explosive temper—is that love?

Loving sinners is messy. Easy answers often elude us. The trouble is, we are all sinners, so if we're going to be the family of God together, we're going to have to deal with each other's sin. In session 5 we'll talk about loving those who sin against you personally. This session is about how to relate to those who sin against others or God.

3. Read John 8:1–11. With what words and actions did Jesus show love for the adulteress?

4. Read the study notes on verses 3 and 6. What sins were the woman's accusers guilty of?

5. Was Jesus "soft on sin"? What in the text makes you say yes or no?

6. In Jesus' day, most husbands would instantly divorce an adulterous wife, leaving her with almost no job opportunities. What do you think Jesus would do if he met this woman six months later and she was someone's mistress?

7. How do you believe members of a Christian community today should relate to a member who engages in persistent sin, such as a pornography addiction or an explosive temper?

8. Read one or more of the following passages, and discuss how it affects your answer to question 7.

   • Jesus warns against judging others in Matthew 7:1–5.
   • Jesus talks about sin in God's family in Matthew 18:15–35.
   • Paul takes a hard line with a sinner in 1 Corinthians 5:1–13.
   • Paul urges restoration for a sinner in 2 Corinthians 2:5–11.

9. Most of us have a mental list of sins that we can overlook in people and a list of sins that really bother us. What's a sin that greatly bothers you?

What would it take for you to love a person who committed that sin the way Jesus loved the adulteress, without condoning the sin?

10. Here's something you can do on your own this week to bring this Bible study home: journal about how God has loved you despite your sin. Write some of your most recent sins, and express gratitude for God's forgiveness. Thank him for the chance to try again with his help. Imagine Jesus looking at you with love and understanding, as he looked at the adulteress when they were alone at the end of the story. He knows everything you've done, and why. He doesn't condone your faults, but he offers you forgiveness and a chance to become who you were meant to be.

   Then phone your spiritual partner. Tell him or her about the sin you wrote about. Ask your partner to support you in prayer about this issue. This may be a scary step, but if your partner is trustworthy, telling someone about your struggle will launch you out of the cycle of sin-and-remorse.

   And if you get a call like this from your partner, remember how Jesus dealt with struggling people!

FOR DEEPER STUDY

Examine the passages in question 8. How would Jesus have you deal with sinners today?

Look at the law for evidence in a legal trial in Deuteronomy 17:6–7. How was it applied, or not applied, in the case of the woman in John 8? Realistically, what would it take to convict someone of adultery by this standard?

Compare Jesus' response to sinners in John 3:17 and John 5:1–15 to what you see in John 8:1–11. What was Jesus' way of dealing with sin and sinners? Would you say from these passages that he was soft on sin? Why or why not?

DEVELOPING YOUR GIFTS TO SERVE OTHERS   10–20 min.

If our model for connections is Jesus' habit of sacrificing for the good of others, then we need to go way beyond coffee and small talk! Below are some more ways to develop deep, sacrificial love for one another.

11. Ask for volunteers to take on some of these ways to serve your group:

☐ (One or two volunteers) Plan a social time outside your group meeting. It can be simple or more ambitious, depending on your group's stage of development. If your group is new, you could go out for ice cream or have a picnic that includes whole families. If your group has been together for some time, take the next step: a camping trip, a formal event, or separate guys-only and girls-only events. Who in your group is good at throwing parties or planning trips? A couple of volunteers can team up to make this happen before or shortly after you reach session 6 of this study.

☐ (*One or two volunteers*) During the week, check in with group members who were absent or who had special prayer requests. This doesn't have to be the leader's job— it just needs one or two people who want to grow in their care for others and who are willing to make a few phone calls. You could take this on for a month and then rotate the role to someone else.

☐ (*One or two volunteers*) If a group member has shared a significant prayer request, such as a job loss or an illness in the family, ask this person how the group can help. You may want to ask privately and then phone group members to organize a response.

Does one person lead all of your group discussions? If so, we encourage you to try rotating leadership. Sign up three group members to lead the three remaining sessions in this study. You can also rotate hosts by meeting in different homes or taking turns providing the refreshments. Use the Small Group Calendar on page 82 to keep track of who will do what.

We encourage rotating leadership so strongly because we've seen people grow dramatically when they take on even a small leadership role. Nobody learns the Bible passage better than the person who guides the discussion!

If you've agreed to one of these tasks, or another way to serve your group, turn to your Personal Health Plan on pages 24–25. Write down the step you're going to take under "WHERE are you serving?"

 SURRENDERING YOUR LIFE FOR GOD'S PLEASURE   15–30 min.

12. Surrendering your heart to God isn't easy. But once we take that area of sin, temptation, disappointment, anxiety, sadness, or anger before the Father, first in private and then into community, we have resources for dealing with that struggle.

Take a moment of quiet reflection to write your thoughts on page 43. Finish this sentence: "Father, I need your help today with . . ."

If you're willing, share what you wrote with your partner, friend, or spouse. The Bible says that bearing one another's burdens is a pathway to healing and hope.

STUDY NOTES

What do you think his disciples thought as Jesus released a lawfully condemned sinner? She was caught in the act. Jesus was a rabbi of second chances. No other rabbi in Palestine was teaching this kind of love that transforms hearts and builds relationships.

Caught in adultery (John 8:3). Jewish law declared that adulterers—both parties in the act—should receive the death penalty (Leviticus 20:10; Deuteronomy 22:22). Here, however, the accusers brought only the woman to Jesus. Where was the man? It was not possible that the man's identity was unknown because Jewish law also required two witnesses to see the physical act in order for persons to be convicted of adultery (Deuteronomy 17:6). Not surprisingly, it was rare for anyone to be charged with this capital offense because two witnesses rarely saw the deed. Furthermore, the accused had a right to a formal trial and execution, not a lynch mob with stones in a public place like the temple. All these facts, plus the strange absence of her husband, suggest that the woman was set up.

Trap (8:6). If Jesus refused to intervene, the lynch mob would stone the woman and ordinary people would blame Jesus. His teachings about mercy would lose all credibility. However, if he said she shouldn't be killed, then the authorities might be able to charge him with teaching against the clear biblical laws.

Wrote on the ground (8:8). Nobody knows what Jesus wrote on the ground. Did he write out their sins? Some think that as the elders saw their own sins made public, they hastily left judgment to someone other than themselves. Or was Jesus just doodling? We don't know. We do know that not one person in the mob could claim to be sinless. That would have denied even what they believed about themselves based on the Old Testament.

PRAYER AND PRAISE REPORT

Briefly share your prayer requests with the large group, making notations below. Then gather in smaller groups of two to four to pray for each other.

Date: _____

Prayer Requests

_____

_____

_____

_____

_____

_____

_____

_____

_____

Praise Report

_____

_____

_____

_____

_____

_____

_____

_____

_____

_____

REFLECTIONS

Use this page to write out your prayers, your thoughts about your daily Bible reading, or your meditations on a verse from the passage you have already studied. Below are some suggested verses for meditation. The Bible Reading Plan is on pages 93–94.

For Meditation: John 8:7 or 8:11

For Gospel Reading:

- What do I *learn* from the life of Christ (his identity, personality, priorities)?

- How does he want me to *live* differently?

_____

_____

_____

_____

_____

_____

_____

_____

_____

_____

_____

_____

_____

_____

_____

_____

_____

_____

DVD NOTES

If you are watching the accompanying *Connecting in Christ Together* DVD, write down what you sense God is saying to you through the speaker. (If you'd like to hear a sample of the DVD teaching segment, go to www.life-together.com/ExperiencingChristTogether.)

_____

_____

_____

_____

_____

_____

_____

_____

_____

_____

_____

_____

_____

_____

_____

_____

_____

_____

_____

_____

_____

_____

_____

_____

_____

_____

TRUTHFUL BUT TENDER

Things had always come easily for Jeff: grades, friends, jobs, money. He took over a failed computer business and by age thirty-five had a Ferrari, a 7,000-square-foot home, a lake house, boats, and more. But more was never enough.

For Jeff and his wife, Liz, the good life included serious drinking. Their church involvement was limited to Sunday services and hefty tithes. But when their pastor encouraged the congregation to join small groups, Jeff and Liz gave it a try. After some detours, they landed in a group that fit them.

Then the good life started to go bad. Their business lost a million-dollar lawsuit. To escape, they spent more time at their lake house and less time at work. Competitors leached away their customers, and eventually their lender forced them to sell their business just as the NASDAQ stock market was crashing. Suddenly Jeff was unemployed, but he didn't care. He had time to goof off and drink. But eighteen months later, the job market was still terrible.

Their small group kept encouraging them to cut down their expensive lifestyle and quit drinking, but Jeff wouldn't listen. Eventually, Jeff and Liz had to file bankruptcy and lost everything. Jeff finally got a job and cut down on spending, but the drinking continued. He was sure that yesterday's success was just around the corner, but great jobs kept barely passing him by. He was spending more time with God and volunteering at church, but God kept withholding financial success. Finally, his men's group confronted him. They told him he needed to give up his drinking and refused to take no for an answer. Jeff decided that if these men he trusted so much felt this way, he would quit then and there. Liz agreed to do the same.

Their life hasn't been perfect since then, but it has improved. Their perspective on what they value has improved. Alcohol no longer clouds Jeff's memory. He has a job he loves that isn't driven by money. He appreciates what he has instead of always wanting more. God has blessed him, and his small group's loving and persistent honesty has been crucial.

CONNECTING WITH GOD'S FAMILY   10 min.

This session explores the tension many of us feel between telling others what we really think and not wanting to hurt their feelings or make them angry. To begin the conversation, you may let everyone share his or her own tendencies in this area (question 1) or let partners check in with each other (question 2).

1. Which of the following best describes you?

   ☐ If I see someone doing something wrong, it's important to me to be truthful, even if it means not always being tactful.

   ☐ If I see someone doing something wrong, it's important to me to deal with the situation tactfully, even if I need to compromise the whole truth.

   Or,

2. Check in with your spiritual partner(s). What are you learning from your personal time with God? How can you support each other in following Christ? (If your partner is absent, join another individual or pair.)

GROWING TO BE LIKE CHRIST   30–40 min.

Jesus didn't just tell people what they wanted to hear. He told them what they needed to hear. Sometimes that made them mad.

Depending on our temperaments, most of us have one of two tendencies when it comes to telling the truth as we see it. Some of us lean toward *niceness*. We want people to feel good; we don't want to hurt anybody's feelings; we may even be uncomfortable with conflict. Others of us lean toward *toughness*. We're blunt, sometimes to the point of being insensitive to people's feelings or differing points of view. Jesus calls us to be honest but not mean, truthful but tender.

Groups where the norm is niceness aren't safe. People feel they have to hide their true thoughts and feelings and just go along with whatever the strongest personalities in the group think and do. Groups with unrestrained toughness aren't safe either. Gentler personalities withdraw to avoid being beaten down.

Jesus made his group of disciples a safe place to grow by being extremely truthful and extremely tender with them. In this study, you're going to look at something Jesus *did* and then at something he *taught* about this subject.

3. Read Matthew 16:13–28. Why did Jesus praise Simon Peter so highly in verses 17–19?

4. How would you feel if you were Peter and Jesus said this to you?

5. Some time later, Peter expressed shock and horror when Jesus foretold what lay ahead for him (verses 21–22). Why do you suppose Peter was so horrified?

6. How would you respond if someone said to you what Jesus says to Peter in verse 23?

7. Can you imagine yourself rebuking someone that forcefully? Why or why not?

8. Why did Jesus think such strong words were necessary (verses 24–28)?

9. In session 3 you saw how Jesus dealt with an adulteress—with tenderness and forgiveness, yet an exhortation to leave her sin behind. Now you've seen how he confronted Peter—not so much tenderness in this scene! Why do you think Jesus was tougher on Peter than on the adulteress?

10. In his teaching, Jesus stressed the *attitudes* we need to have before we consider confronting someone. What attitude does he emphasize in Matthew 7:1–5? (You may want to consult the Study Notes.)

    Why is this attitude essential when we're telling someone a hard truth?

11. What attitude does he emphasize in Matthew 5:21–22? Why is this attitude essential?

12. What's the difference between the judging he warns against in Matthew 7:1–5 and what he does in Matthew 16:23?

13. How do you think this discussion will affect how you respond when someone does something you think is wrong?

FOR DEEPER STUDY

Read Luke 22:31–34, another conversation between Simon Peter and Jesus. How tough or tender is Jesus now?

How tough or tender with Peter is Jesus in John 21:15–19, after Peter denied Jesus three times? After looking at several passages showing Jesus' interactions with Peter, what conclusions do you draw about how he dealt with this friend?

What else can we learn about confronting people from Galatians 6:1–5 and Romans 14:1–13?

 DEVELOPING YOUR GIFTS TO SERVE OTHERS   15 min.

14. Role-playing is a good way to take relational issues out of the realm of theory. Gather into smaller circles of three or four people for this exercise.

☐ Ask for a volunteer in your circle to play the role of a group member who frequently directs barbed comments at other members. This person claims that his or her comments are meant in fun, mere teasing, but others find the comments hurtful.

☐ Ask for another volunteer in your circle to play the role of a member who decides to go to this person in private to ask him or her to stop this behavior. The confronter should try to be truthful but kind, even if the person being confronted becomes defensive. Keep in mind both Jesus' example and his teaching. Be honest, but avoid letting anger or a judgmental attitude color your words.

The others in your circle will be observers. Give the two volunteers five minutes to play out their conversation. Then discuss together what worked well and what could be improved. Remember to be both truthful and tender in evaluating each other!

SURRENDERING YOUR LIFE FOR GOD'S PLEASURE 15–30 min.

15. Stay with your smaller circles for prayer. How can they pray for you this week?

16. If you have the LIFE TOGETHER Worship DVD/CD or another worship CD, complete this session with one of the slower songs. The first time through, listen without singing, possibly with your eyes closed. Play the song again and quietly sing to the Father as a prayer. Don't worry about anyone else but God. Draw near to God and he will draw near to you.

STUDY NOTES

John the Baptist . . . Elijah . . . one of the prophets (Matthew 16:14). People were talking about Jesus' identity. Was he like one of the Old Testament prophets? Was he Elijah, who went to heaven without dying and was prophesied to return (2 Kings 2:1–12; Malachi 4:5–6)? King Herod believed he was John the Baptist raised from the dead (Matthew 14:2).

You are the Christ, the Son of the living God (16:16). Christ (Greek) = *Messiah* (Hebrew) = Anointed One. That is, the prophet/king/deliverer whom the Old Testament said God would send. "Son of the living God" went further, implying not just authority but divinity.

On this rock I will build my church (16:18). This is one of Jesus' most hotly debated statements. Was the rock Peter (*Petros* in Greek means "little rock")? Or was it his statement of faith about Christ? What was rocklike that formed the foundation of the church? While there are commentators on both sides of this issue, we believe Jesus affirmed both Peter and his statement. The closest antecedent to "this rock" is "Peter." So Peter and his confession of faith formed the foundation of the early church. And in fact, Peter became a leader of the early church and often was a spokesman for the apostles (Acts 2:14).

Keys of the kingdom (16:19). Christ gave his followers the authority to lead others to faith based upon confessing Jesus as the Christ, the son of the living God.

Get behind me, Satan! (16:23). Jesus didn't mean Peter was Satan but that his comment was influenced by Satan. Apparently, to think from a human perspective ("have in mind . . . the things of men") rather than God's perspective ("the things of God") was so wrong in this situation that it called for the strongest language. Unwittingly, by urging Jesus to avoid the cross, Peter was doing something that served the Devil.

All good relationships are founded on honesty. Jesus never protected his followers from the truth about himself or his mission. Peter felt the freedom to say what he thought, and Jesus was frank about his response. These men were at a point in their relationship where they didn't need to mince words.

Judge (Matthew 7:1–2). Jesus isn't telling us not to exercise discernment or form opinions about people's character. In fact, a few paragraphs later in Matthew 7:15–20, he tells us to recognize untrustworthy teachers and leaders by assessing the fruit of their lives. In other words, by exercising good judgment. But the Greek word Jesus uses in 7:1–2 has the flavor of a court in which a judge passes sentence. The parallel passage in Luke 6:37 amplifies what Jesus meant: "Do not condemn, and you will not be condemned." We are right to have opinions about the rightness or wrongness of what someone else does. We are right to use discernment in trusting someone or withholding trust. But we are wrong to claim the right to pass final sentence on someone. Discernment is good, but arrogance, harshness, and condemnation are not. It's sometimes necessary to confront someone about a behavior we believe is wrong. But we should do so gently, humbly aware that we too are potential wrongdoers (Galatians 6:1–3). Further, some issues aren't black and white but matters of personal conscience best left to God (Romans 14:1–13).

PRAYER AND PRAISE REPORT

Briefly share your prayer requests with the large group, making notations below. Then gather in smaller groups of two to four to pray for each other.

Date: _____

Prayer Requests

_____

_____

_____

_____

_____

_____

_____

_____

_____

Praise Report

_____

_____

_____

_____

_____

_____

_____

_____

_____

REFLECTIONS

Use this page to write out your prayers, your thoughts about your daily Bible reading, or your meditations on a verse from the passage you have already studied. Below are some suggested verses for meditation. The Bible Reading Plan is on pages 93–94.

For Meditation: Matthew 7:1–2 or 16:23

For Gospel Reading:

- What do I *learn* from the life of Christ (his identity, personality, priorities)?

- How does he want me to *live* differently?

DVD NOTES

If you are watching the accompanying *Connecting in Christ Together* DVD, write down what you sense God is saying to you through the speaker. (If you'd like to hear a sample of the DVD teaching segment, go to www.life-together.com/ExperiencingChristTogether.)

_____

_____

_____

_____

_____

_____

_____

_____

_____

_____

_____

_____

_____

_____

_____

_____

_____

_____

_____

_____

_____

_____

_____

_____

EXTREME FORGIVENESS

Tom sobbed when he heard his wife's words: "I found another man and I am leaving you."

Through his tears he said, "I forgive you, Monica, but I don't trust you."

Monica wanted to be released without a fight. But Tom wouldn't let her go—he loved her more than that. Over many agonizing months, Monica first left the other man to repair her marriage, and then was unfaithful again.

Tom told her she had to leave the house until she was willing to work on the marriage. Again Monica decided to commit to Tom and leave the other man.

One night she told Tom she was pregnant, and it wasn't Tom's baby. It was more than Tom could bear. He struggled month after month, wondering whether he should leave his wife. He couldn't bear the thought of raising someone else's baby.

With five weeks left in the pregnancy, he decided to leave her. During a Bible study, Tom's small group leader challenged his decision. "Tom," he said, "this baby is not some other man's. It's God's baby, and he wants you to raise it with your wife. Leave the rest to God."

Tom went home and told Monica he was committed to her and the baby. When Jacob was born, the other man came to see the child. Tom prayed to be able to love this man with Christ's love. He prayed the whole way to the hospital. When he walked in, he told the man, "Hey, enjoy the baby. Go ahead and hold him."

The man had brought two large buddies, thinking the scene might get ugly. But it didn't. A few days later, he phoned and asked to speak with Tom. He told Tom that never in his life had he met anyone who had handled himself in such a way. "I don't understand your Christian thing," he said, "but I am half the man you are. I want you to raise this child. You will do twice the job I could do."

A blood test later revealed that it wasn't the other man's baby after all. But even if the test had turned out otherwise, Tom knew he'd done what Jesus would want.

CONNECTING WITH GOD'S FAMILY 10 min.

Choose one of these two openers:

1. If a reporter came to your group and watched for a few weeks, what would he or she say is the most bizarre thing about your group? What would he or she say is the best thing?

Or,

2. Check in with your spiritual partner(s). Share something you wrote in your journal. How can you encourage each other in your personal connections with Christ?

GROWING TO BE LIKE CHRIST 30–40 min.

Nothing in Jesus' teaching seems more outrageous to many readers than his ideas about forgiveness and loving enemies. Some think his idea of love is highly practical and rational, while others think it's too idealistic in our rough-and-tumble world.

But Jesus practiced what he preached. He loved his enemies in a world where "enemies" included ruthless soldiers, corrupt government officials, and hypocritical religious leaders. His stance got him killed, but it also achieved his ultimate goals.

3. Read Luke 6:27–38. Which of these instructions seem hard for you to practice day to day?

4. What reasons did Jesus give for living this way?

5. Compare Luke 6:29, Jesus' teaching about turning the other cheek, to John 18:19–24, the passage describing when Jesus was struck in the face following his arrest. What can we learn from his actions about what turning the other cheek means and doesn't mean? (You may want to consult the Study Notes as well.)

6. How realistic do you think it is for you, in your circumstances, to turn the other cheek or do good to those who treat you badly? Please explain.

7. Luke 23:33–34 describes how Jesus responded to the people who were brutally killing him. What motivated him to respond like this?

8. How do you react to Jesus' model? For instance, are you thinking, "I want to be like that" or "That's great for him, but I don't want to get crucified"?

9. Think of someone who has hurt you. What will it take for you to treat that person with love?

10. How do you think Jesus would tell you to deal with a person who will take advantage of you if you don't stand up for yourself?

FOR DEEPER STUDY

Read Luke 17:3–4. What guidelines for forgiveness does Jesus offer here?

What do you think Jesus would say about dealing with an ex-spouse or ex-girfriend/boyfriend? Responding to a spouse who repeatedly hurts you in the same way? Dealing with a rude and disobedient teenager? Responding to a parent who speaks words that tear you down? Dealing with a coworker who undercuts you? Suing a doctor for medical malpractice?

What does Paul say in Romans 12:9–21 about loving one's enemies? How do his views explain or expand on Jesus' words?

In Ephesians 4:25–5:2, Paul discusses some related attitudes he saw as essential for a Christian community. What are those attitudes?

Why do you think both Jesus and Paul treated anger and forgiveness as such core issues that Christians simply have to deal with? How realistic do you think their ideas are for your situation?

SHARING YOUR LIFE MISSION EVERY DAY　　　　15 min.

One of the best things you can do to strengthen the connections within your group is to give away some of what you've received. Below are a couple of options for you to consider.

11. Take your group to a deeper level by doing a service project for people outside your group. Who would be willing to team up to plan a service project over the next three months? You can visit someone in the hospital. Bring a meal to someone who is ill. Do chores for someone who is overwhelmed. Rake leaves or shovel snow for an elderly person. Your pastor may have additional ideas. We've seen unbelievers decide to investigate faith in Christ just because a group visited them in the hospital. Groups who get out of their living rooms at least four times a year to serve others gain much more intimacy and personal growth than those who do Bible study alone.

12. If this study has helped you deepen your connection with Christ and one another, we encourage you to share it with others. The best way to plant the good news of Christ deep in your heart is to give it away. Maybe you have one friend with whom you could meet one-on-one to go through either this study or the first book in the series, *Beginning in Christ Together*.

Or, maybe your pastor could use your help in starting new small groups. If so, you could take a six-week break from your group to lead a new group through this study. During that time, you can coach one of the group members to take over leadership. After six weeks, you return to this group.

In Jesus' kingdom, the more you give away, the more you have. Take a moment to think about how you can give away what you've gained in this group. On the Personal Health Plan on page 24, write down the step you plan to take under "WHEN are shepherding another in Christ?"

13. Who are the volunteers who agreed in session 3 to plan a group social event? Ask them to update the group on their plans and recruit help if necessary.

SURRENDERING YOUR LIFE FOR GOD'S PLEASURE 15–30 min.

14. Gather with one or two group members to form a smaller circle. Together pray about forgiveness—either a situation in which you need God's help to forgive someone or an area where you need God's forgiveness. In what area of your life do you most need God to work? If you are comfortable doing so, you may want to lay a hand on a person's shoulder as you pray for him or her.

15. Plan a special time of worship to end session 6. Among the possibilities, you could listen to music from the DVD or the LIFE TOGETHER Worship DVD/CD series, sing together, or read psalms.

    Session 6 takes a close look at the cross as a model for Christian love. It would be a great time to share Communion or the Lord's Supper together. Communion remembers and honors Christ for offering his life for you. How does your church do Communion?

    Consider planning a time to share Communion together. Ask your pastor for guidance. You may also go to www.lifetogether.com for a free download of instructions for sharing Communion in a small group. Are there one or two group members who would be willing to plan your worship as you complete this study?

STUDY NOTES

The instructions in Luke 6:27–38 are not meant to be understood as legalistic. Jesus is not saying, "Every time someone takes something that belongs to you, you *must* let them have it." Rather, he is giving examples of behavior that becomes typical as we experience God's love for us and see others through his eyes. These are the habits of a heart that understands what's really important in life. There will be times when the most loving way to respond to someone is to say no to him. But because anger, fear, and obsession with our own rights and possessions no longer control us, our natural response to personal injury will be good rather than evil.

It takes time for us to grow into these habits, but they're entirely practical and realistic. Luke addressed his gospel to a group of small churches with economically and politically threatened members. By applying these principles for three centuries, these communities grew to the point where their faith dominated the entire Roman Empire. The unusual quality of Christian love was one of the chief factors in conversions during that period.

Love (Luke 6:27, 32, 35). To love someone is to will (desire, choose, intend, pursue) good for her. Love doesn't require that we enjoy someone's company or trust her with our secrets. Yet even if we know her flaws, we can ask ourselves, "What is in this person's best interest? How can I contribute to that?" The very act of exploring such questions gives God space to work in our hearts.

Turn to him the other [cheek] (6:29). To turn the other cheek is to remain vulnerable. It is to be more concerned with doing good than with protecting ourselves or striking back. The person who turns the other cheek knows his worth in God's eyes and has delivered all fears into God's hands. When he draws the line, he does so without malice and with the abuser's best interests at heart.

For example, a battered woman isn't turning the other cheek when she fearfully tolerates abuse. She turns the other cheek when she calmly points out the injustice of the abuse (as Jesus did in John 18:22–23; see below). She turns the other cheek when she leaves her abuser, taking her children with her, for the good of the children and for the abuser's ultimate good as well. Some battered women ultimately resort to violently attacking their abusers out of self-defense; Jesus would want them to seek every means of escape before getting to that point.

Jesus never tells us to turn someone else's cheek. We should never shut our eyes to abuse directed at someone else, but should intervene out of love for all persons involved.

Do not stop him from taking your tunic (6:29). This might seem like a passive response to someone taking advantage of you. But in fact, it's a way to seize the initiative. You're no longer a victim; you're extending yourself in generous love.

This verse also is relevant to legal cases. While Jesus doesn't forbid us from seeking justice, he does ask us to run all lawsuits through a grid that asks, "What is good for the other party?" not just "What is good for me?"

Jesus himself often said no to people (see Luke 4:42–44, for example). Boundaries are good. But Jesus wanted us to let love rather than self-focus shape our boundaries.

Struck him (John 18:22). An officer of the court struck Jesus. This was an illegal act of abuse to an uncondemned prisoner. Yet instead of pressing charges (or calling down a legion of angels to punish the wrongdoers), Jesus challenged the officer to examine himself (see verse 23). Jesus focused not on getting out of this situation alive, nor on seeing his enemies punished. He did the most loving thing he could do for this officer—challenge him to consider the justice of his actions.

Seven times (Luke 17:4). "It is not likely that a believer would commit the same sin seven times in one day, but we must be ready to forgive that often. Forgiveness should be a habit, not a battle."[3]

---

[3]Warren W. Wiersbe, "Expository Outlines of the New Testament," in *The Bible Exposition Commentary* (Wheaton, Ill.: SP Publications, Inc., 1989). PC Study Bible Version 3.2, July 2001.

PRAYER AND PRAISE REPORT

Briefly share your prayer requests with the large group, making notations below. Then gather in smaller groups of two to four to pray for each other.

Date: _____

Prayer Requests

_____

_____

_____

_____

_____

_____

_____

_____

_____

_____

Praise Report

_____

_____

_____

_____

_____

_____

_____

_____

_____

_____

_____

_____

REFLECTIONS

Use this page to write out your prayers, your thoughts about your daily Bible reading, or your meditations on a verse from the passage you have already studied. Below are some suggested verses for meditation. The Bible Reading Plan is on pages 93–94.

For Meditation: Luke 6:27 or 6:35–36

For Gospel Reading:

- What do I *learn* from the life of Christ (his identity, personality, priorities)?

- How does he want me to *live* differently?

DVD NOTES

If you are watching the accompanying *Connecting in Christ Together* DVD, write down what you sense God is saying to you through the speaker. (If you'd like to hear a sample of the DVD teaching segment, go to www.life-together.com/ExperiencingChristTogether.)

6 CROSS-SHAPED LOVE

Living with an addict had become part of Susan's everyday life. Often by just looking into Mark's eyes as he walked in the door, she knew he was loaded. Disappointment, mistrust, and anger seeped deep into her heart.

When Mark returned from his third rehab center and decided to commit his life to the Lord, Susan felt nothing. She had been through it so many times before that she didn't have the reserve left to believe that God could change him. Susan had grown up somewhat religious but had never experienced Christ's work on the cross for *her* sin and his forgiveness for *her* imperfections.

But when Mark returned to drugs yet again, Susan began to read the Bible and understand Christ's love for her. Jesus' love softened her; she felt awe that he had died for her. She realized that while Mark's behavior was unacceptable, her own bitterness was equally sinful. Coming face to face with Christ freed her to forgive Mark for all the pain she had endured over the years. To love Mark, she knew she needed a motivation beyond herself, and she found it in the cross.

Susan's decision to love Mark as Christ loved her couldn't control Mark's behavior. He sank deeper into drugs and eventually abandoned their marriage. Embracing the cross didn't guarantee a happy ending. But it did enable Susan to love Mark with truth and tenderness, and then go forward in life without bitterness. In this final session, you'll explore what motivation for love you find in Jesus' sacrifice.

CONNECTING WITH GOD'S FAMILY   10 min.

1. In a couple of sentences, describe one situation this week in which you were challenged to love.

   Or,

2. Check in with your spiritual partner(s). As you look back over the past month, what is one of the main things God has been teaching you through your personal time with him?

GROWING TO BE LIKE CHRIST   30–40 min.

Jesus knew his disciples wouldn't love each other just because he told them to. They needed to see him demonstrate extreme love for them. We too are unlikely to love one another just because we read about love in the Bible. We need to know, deep down, that Jesus loves us with total, sacrificial love. We need to experience being loved.

Sometimes the knowledge that Jesus died for us becomes distant, abstract. We need this knowledge to be vivid, at the front of our minds. That's why Jesus repeated, "as I have loved you." The more we look hard at the cross, making it the lens through which we see life, the more "love one another as I have loved you" will become our natural response to people.

3. Read Matthew 27:32–56. If you had been present at Christ's crucifixion, what would you have seen? Describe as many sights as possible.

4. If you had been there, what would you have heard? Describe as many sounds as possible.

5. What makes this event an act of love, not just a gruesome tragedy? See some or all of the following:

- Hebrews 2:14–15
- Hebrews 9:13–15
- Colossians 2:13–15
- Romans 5:9–11

6. Why do you suppose Matthew detailed the insults Jesus received while he was dying (Matthew 27:39–44)?

7. Why did the Father separate himself from Jesus while he was on the cross (Matthew 27:46)? See the last study note (page 73), and try to explain this in your own words.

8. Jesus died to cleanse us from our sins, especially our failure to love God and others as we should. Think back over what you've learned about love throughout this study:

- Laying down your life for another person
- Showing up and taking action for someone in need
- Treating a sinful person with warmth instead of condemnation
- Telling someone a hard truth with a tender heart
- Forgiving someone who harms you

On the Reflections page (page 75), write the name of one person you have recently failed to love as well as you should, perhaps in one of these ways. You won't have to share this name with the group unless you want to.

9. What difference does it make to you that God has forgiven the failure you noted in question 8?

10. To what extent does Christ's love for you—his sacrifice for you in your need, his forgiveness of your sins, his care instead of condemnation—motivate you to love others? Does it motivate you a lot, or not much? Why do you think that is?

11. How would you like this study, and this group experience, to affect the way you handle relationships from now on?

FOR DEEPER STUDY

Compare Psalm 22 to Jesus' experience on the cross. Other than the first verse, what other verses reflect what Jesus may have been thinking?

Read Romans 3:21–31. Why does Jesus' death "justify" us—that is, make God declare us not guilty of our sins?

Read Philippians 2:1–13. How did Paul think the cross should affect the way you live day to day?

What parallels do you see between Isaiah's prophecy of the suffering servant (Isaiah 52:13–53:12) and what actually happened to Jesus?

For the Old Testament background on the idea of sacrifice for sin, see Leviticus 16. What was the point of blood sacrifice?

SHARING YOUR LIFE MISSION EVERY DAY 15–20 min.

12. What's next for your group? Do you want to continue meeting together? If so, the LIFE TOGETHER Agreement on pages 80–81 can help you talk through what you want to do the same and what you want to do differently as you move forward. What will you study? Perhaps another book in this series?

13. Is anyone in your group willing to take a six-week break to lead a new group through a LIFE TOGETHER study? If even one or two of your group members are willing to take up the challenge of leadership, that's something to celebrate!

   Gather around them and ask them to share their greatest fear as they go out to lead. Then pray for them, asking God's abundant blessing on their commitment. And don't worry: they'll be back once the new group gets off the ground.

SURRENDERING YOUR LIFE FOR GOD'S PLEASURE 15–30 min.

14. The Bible says, "The prayers of a righteous man are powerful and effective." How has God answered your prayers during this study? Review past Prayer and Praise Reports and update the group on answered prayers.

15. Close this session with worship and celebration that focus on Christ crucified for you. Here are some ideas:

☐ Play one or two songs that focus on Christ's sacrifice or God's goodness. Listen to the song once worshipfully, then play the song again and sing with it.

☐ Share Communion or the Lord's Supper together.

STUDY NOTES

Jesus suffered the death that we earned through our sins. Some of us have trouble being gripped by that idea. We feel that while we have faults, we've done nothing that deserves death. It's helpful, then, to consider how serious our sins are.

Our fundamental sin is lack of love. The opposite of love can be hatred or merely indifference. Lovelessness can just be not doing what we could and should do for other people's good. Lack of love toward God can be not caring enough to be intimate with him. Or not caring whether he receives the worship that his magnificent goodness deserves.

God is utterly loving. He's also *holy*. Holiness is a quality that makes it impossible for someone loveless to be alive in God's presence. Lovelessness and God just don't mix. The person dies. But as we've seen throughout this study, love is hard. Who among us loves well enough? Thus, our only hope for life in God's presence is for Jesus to take all our wretched lovelessness on himself and suffer death in our place. Then we take his love into us and become what we couldn't be on our own.

Crucified (Matthew 27:35). "Crucifixion was one of the most cruel and barbarous forms of death known to man. . . . So dreaded was it that even in the pre-Christian era, the cares and troubles of life were often compared to a cross. The agony of the crucified victim was brought about by (1) the painful but nonfatal character of the wounds inflicted, (2) the abnormal position of the body, the slightest movement causing additional torture, and (3) the traumatic fever induced by hanging for such a long period of time. . . . When a person is suspended by his two hands, the blood sinks rapidly into the lower extremities of the body. Within six to twelve minutes the blood pressure has dropped to half, while the rate of the pulse has doubled. The heart is deprived of blood, and fainting follows. Death during crucifixion is due to heart failure. Victims of crucifixion did not generally succumb for two or three days. Death was hastened by the 'crucifragium' or the breaking of the legs. 'But when they came to Jesus and found that he was already dead, they did not break his legs' (John 19:33)."[4]

My God, my God, why have you forsaken me? (27:46). Jesus was quoting Psalm 22:1. In that moment, Jesus bore the sins of the world upon himself. His Father had to forsake him because of the sin. It was agonizing for Jesus to be separated from his Father—in all eternity he had never experienced this. Psalm 22 as a whole includes affirmations of faith despite suffering.

---

[4]"Cross," *New International Bible Dictionary*, in *The Zondervan Bible Study Library* CD-ROM, version 5.0 (Grand Rapids: Zondervan, 2003).

PRAYER AND PRAISE REPORT

Briefly share your prayer requests with the large group, making notations below. Then gather in smaller groups of two to four to pray for each other.

Date: _____

Prayer Requests

_____

_____

_____

_____

_____

_____

_____

_____

_____

Praise Report

_____

_____

_____

_____

_____

_____

_____

_____

_____

_____

REFLECTIONS

Use this page to write out your prayers, your thoughts about your daily Bible reading, or your meditations on a verse from the passage you have already studied. Below are some suggested verses for meditation. The Bible Reading Plan is on pages 93–94.

For Meditation: Matthew 27:41–44 or 27:45–46

For Gospel Reading:

- What do I *learn* from the life of Christ (his identity, personality, priorities)?

- How does he want me to *live* differently?

_____

_____

_____

_____

_____

_____

_____

_____

_____

_____

_____

_____

_____

_____

_____

_____

_____

_____

DVD NOTES

If you are watching the accompanying *Connecting in Christ Together* DVD, write down what you sense God is saying to you through the speaker. (If you'd like to hear a sample of the DVD teaching segment, go to www.life-together.com/ExperiencingChristTogether.)

_____

_____

_____

_____

_____

_____

_____

_____

_____

_____

_____

_____

_____

_____

_____

_____

_____

_____

_____

_____

_____

_____

_____

_____

FREQUENTLY ASKED QUESTIONS

What do we do on the first night of our group?

Like all fun things in life—have a party! A "get to know you" coffee, dinner, or dessert is a great way to launch a new study. You may want to review the LIFE TOGETHER Agreement (pages 80–81) and share the names of a few friends you can invite to join you. But most importantly, have fun before your study time begins.

Where do we find new members for our group?

This can be troubling, especially for new groups that have only a few people or for existing groups that lose a few people along the way. We encourage you to pray with your group and then brainstorm a list of people from work, church, your neighborhood, your children's school, family, the gym, and so forth. Then have each group member invite several of the people on his or her list. Another good strategy is to ask church leaders to make an announcement or allow a bulletin insert.

No matter how you find members, it's vital that you stay on the lookout for new people to join your group. All groups tend to go through healthy attrition—the result of moves, releasing new leaders, ministry opportunities, and so forth—and if the group gets too small, it could be at risk of shutting down. If you and your group stay open, you'll be amazed at the people God sends your way. The next person just might become a friend for life. You never know!

How long will this group meet?

It's totally up to the group—once you come to the end of this six-week study. Most groups meet weekly for at least the first six weeks, but every other week can work as well. We strongly recommend that the group meet for the first six months on a weekly basis if at all possible. This allows for continuity, and if people miss a meeting they aren't gone for a whole month.

At the end of this study, each group member may decide if he or she wants to continue on for another six-week study. Some groups launch relationships for years to come, and others are stepping-stones into another group experience. Either way, enjoy the journey.

Can we do this study on our own?

Absolutely! This may sound crazy but one of the best ways to do this study is not with a full house but with a few friends. You may choose to gather with one other couple who would enjoy going to the movies or having a quiet dinner and then walking through this study. Jesus will be with you even if there are only two of you (Matthew 18:20).

What if this group is not working for us?

You're not alone! This could be the result of a personality conflict, life stage difference, geographical distance, level of spiritual maturity, or any number of things. Relax. Pray for God's direction, and at the end of this six-week study, decide whether to continue with this group or find another. You don't buy the first car you look at or marry the first person you date, and the same goes with a group. Don't bail out before the six weeks are up—God might have something to teach you. Also, don't run from conflict or prejudge people before you have given them a chance. God is still working in you too!

Who is the leader?

Most groups have an official leader. But ideally, the group will mature and members will rotate the leadership of meetings. We have discovered that healthy groups rotate hosts/leaders and homes on a regular basis. This model ensures that all members grow, give their unique contribution, and develop their gifts. This study guide and the Holy Spirit can keep things on track even when you rotate leaders. Christ has promised to be in your midst as you gather. Ultimately, God is your leader each step of the way.

How do we handle the child care needs in our group?

Very carefully. Seriously, this can be a sensitive issue. We suggest that you empower the group to openly brainstorm solutions. You may try one option that works for a while and then adjust over time. Our favorite approach is for adults to meet in the living room or dining room, and to share the cost of a babysitter (or two) who can be with the kids in a different part of the house. In this way, parents don't have to be away from their children all evening when their children are too young to be left at home. A second option is to use one home for the kids and a second home (close by or a phone call away) for the adults. A third idea is to rotate the responsibility of providing a lesson or care for the children either in the same home or in another home nearby. This can be an incredible blessing for kids. Finally, the most common idea is to decide that you need to have a night to invest in your spiritual lives individually or as a couple, and to make your own arrangements for child care. No matter what decision the group makes, the best approach is to dialogue openly about both the problem and the solution.

To answer your further questions, we have created a website called www.lifetogether.com/ExperiencingChristTogether that can be your small group coach. Here are ten reasons to check out this website:

1. Top twenty questions every new leader asks
2. Common problems most new leaders face and ways to overcome them
3. Seven steps to building a healthy small group in six weeks
4. Free downloadable resources and leadership support
5. Additional leadership training material for every lesson in the EXPERIENCING CHRIST TOGETHER series
6. Ten stories from leaders who successfully completed this study
7. Free chat rooms and bulletin boards
8. Downloadable Health Assessments and Health Plans for individuals or groups
9. A chance to join a community of small group leaders by affinity, geography, or denominational affiliation
10. Best of all, a free newsletter with the best ideas from leaders around the world

LIFE TOGETHER AGREEMENT

APPENDIX

OUR PURPOSE

To transform our spiritual lives by cultivating our spiritual health in a healthy small group community. In addition, we: _____

_____

_____.

OUR VALUES

Group Attendance	To give priority to the group meeting. We will call or email if we will be late or absent. (Completing the Small Group Calendar on page 82 will minimize this issue.)
Safe Environment	To help create a safe place where people can be heard and feel loved. (Please, no quick answers, snap judgments, or simple fixes.)
Respect Differences	To be gentle and gracious to people with different spiritual maturity, personal opinions, temperaments, or imperfections. We are all works in progress.
Confidentiality	To keep anything that is shared strictly confidential and within the group, and to avoid sharing improper information about those outside the group.
Encouragement for Growth	To be not just takers but givers of life. We want to spiritually multiply our life by serving others with our God-given gifts.
Welcome for Newcomers	To keep an open chair and share Jesus' dream of finding a shepherd for every sheep.
Shared Ownership	To remember that every member is a minister and to ensure that each attender will share a

80

small team role or responsibility over time. (See Team Roles on pages 83–85.)

Rotating Hosts/Leaders and Homes To encourage different people to host the group in their homes, and to rotate the responsibility of facilitating each meeting. (See the Small Group Calendar on page 82.)

OUR EXPECTATIONS

• Refreshments/mealtimes _____

• Child care _____

• When we will meet (day of week) _____

• Where we will meet (place) _____

• We will begin at (time)_____ and end at _____

• We will do our best to have some or all of us attend a worship service together. Our primary worship service time will be _____

• Date of this agreement _____

• Date we will review this agreement again _____

• Who (other than the leader) will review this agreement at the end of this study_____

SMALL GROUP CALENDAR

Planning and calendaring can help ensure the greatest participation at every meeting. At the end of each meeting, review this calendar. Be sure to include a regular rotation of host homes and leaders, and don't forget birthdays, socials, church events, holidays, and mission/ministry projects. Go to www.lifetogether.com for an electronic copy of this form and more than a hundred ideas for your group to do together.

Date	Lesson	Host Home	Dessert/Meal	Leader
Monday, January 15	1	Steve and Laura's	Joe	Bill

TEAM ROLES

The Bible makes clear that every member, not just the small group leader, is a minister in the body of Christ. In a healthy small group, every member takes on some small role or responsibility. It's more fun and effective if you team up on these roles.

Review the team roles and responsibilities below, and have each member volunteer for a role or participate on a team. If someone doesn't know where to serve or is holding back, have the group suggest a team or role. It's best to have one or two people on each team so you have each of the five purposes covered. Serving in even a small capacity will not only help your leader but also will make the group more fun for everyone. Don't hold back. Join a team!

The opportunities below are broken down by the five purposes and then by a *crawl* (beginning step), *walk* (intermediate step), or *run* (advanced step). Try to cover at least the crawl and walk roles, and select a role that matches your group, your gifts, and your maturity. If you can't find a good step or just want to see other ideas, go to www.lifetogether.com and see what other groups are choosing.

Team Roles	Team Player(s)

CONNECTING TEAM (Fellowship and Community Building)

Crawl:	Host a social event or group activity in the first week or two.	_____ _____
Walk:	Create a list of uncommitted members and then invite them to an open house or group social.	_____ _____
Run:	Plan a twenty-four-hour retreat or weekend getaway for the group. Lead the Connecting time each week for the group.	_____ _____

GROWING TEAM (Discipleship and Spiritual Growth)

Crawl: Coordinate the spiritual partners for the group. Facilitate a three- or four-person discussion circle during the Bible study portion of your meeting. Coordinate the discussion circles.

_____

_____

Walk: Tabulate the Personal Health Assessments and Health Plans in a summary to let people know how you're doing as a group. Encourage personal devotions through group discussions and pairing up with spiritual (accountability) partners.

_____

_____

Run: Take the group on a prayer walk, or plan a day of solitude, fasting, or personal retreat.

_____

_____

SERVING TEAM (Discovering Your God-Given Design for Ministry)

Crawl: Ensure that every member finds a group role or team he or she enjoys.

_____

_____

Walk: Have every member take a gift test (see www.lifetogether.com) and determine your group's gifts. Plan a ministry project together.

_____

_____

Run: Help each member decide on a way to use his or her unique gifts somewhere in the church.

_____

_____

SHARING TEAM (Sharing and Evangelism)

Crawl: Coordinate the group's Prayer and Praise Report of friends and family who don't know Christ.

_____

_____

Walk: Search for group mission opportunities and plan a cross-cultural group activity.

_____

_____

Run: Take a small-group "vacation" to host a six-week group in your neighborhood or office. Then come back together with your current group.

_____

_____

SURRENDERING TEAM (Surrendering Your Heart to Worship)

Crawl: Maintain the group's Prayer
and Praise Report or journal.

      _____

Walk: Lead a brief time of worship each
week (at the beginning or end of
your meeting), either a cappella or
using a song from the DVD or the
LIFE TOGETHER Worship DVD/CD.

Run: Plan a unique time of worship through
Communion, foot washing, night of
prayer, or nature walking.

PERSONAL HEALTH ASSESSMENT

	Just Beginning	Getting Going	Well Developed

CONNECTING WITH GOD AND OTHERS

I am deepening my understanding of and friendship
with God in community with others.   1 2 3 4 5

I am growing in my ability both to share and to
show my love to others.   1 2 3 4 5

I am willing to share my real needs for prayer and
support from others.   1 2 3 4 5

I am resolving conflict constructively and am
willing to forgive others.   1 2 3 4 5

CONNECTING Total _____

GROWING IN YOUR SPIRITUAL JOURNEY

I have a growing relationship with God through regular
time in the Bible and in prayer (spiritual habits).   1 2 3 4 5

I am experiencing more of the characteristics of
Jesus Christ (love, patience, gentleness, courage,
self-control, and so forth) in my life.   1 2 3 4 5

I am avoiding addictive behaviors (food, television,
busyness, and the like) to meet my needs.   1 2 3 4 5

I am spending time with a Christian friend (spiritual partner)
who celebrates and challenges my spiritual growth.   1 2 3 4 5

GROWING Total _____

SERVING WITH YOUR GOD-GIVEN DESIGN

I have discovered and am further developing my
unique God-given design.   1 2 3 4 5

I am regularly praying for God to show me
opportunities to serve him and others.   1 2 3 4 5

I am serving in a regular (once a month or more)
ministry in the church or community.   1 2 3 4 5

I am a team player in my small group by sharing
some group role or responsibility.   1 2 3 4 5

SERVING Total _____

SHARING GOD'S LOVE IN EVERYDAY LIFE

I am cultivating relationships with non-Christians and praying
for God to give me natural opportunities to share his love.   1 2 3 4 5

I am praying and learning about where God can use me
and my group cross-culturally for missions.   1 2 3 4 5

I am investing my time in another person or group who
needs to know Christ.   1 2 3 4 5

I am regularly inviting unchurched or unconnected
friends to my church or small group.   1 2 3 4 5

SHARING Total _____

SURRENDERING YOUR LIFE TO GOD

I am experiencing more of the presence and
power of God in my everyday life.   1 2 3 4 5

I am faithfully attending services and my
small group to worship God.   1 2 3 4 5

I am seeking to please God by surrendering every
area of my life (health, decisions, finances,
relationships, future, and the like) to him.   1 2 3 4 5

I am accepting the things I cannot change and
becoming increasingly grateful for the life I've been given.   1 2 3 4 5

SURRENDERING Total _____

	Connecting	Growing	Serving	Sharing	Surrendering	
20						Well Developed
16						Very Good
12						Getting Going
8						Fair
4						Just Beginning

○ Beginning Assessment Total _____   ☐ Ending Assessment Total _____

PERSONAL
HEALTH PLAN

This worksheet could become your single most important feature in this study. On it you can record your personal priorities before the Father. It will help you live a healthy spiritual life, balancing all five of God's purposes.

PURPOSE	PLAN
CONNECT	WHO are you connecting with spiritually?
GROW	WHAT is your next step for growth?
DEVELOP	WHERE are you serving?
SHARE	WHEN are you shepherding another in Christ?
SURRENDER	HOW are you surrendering your heart?

Additional copies of the Personal Health Plan may be downloaded in a larger format at www.lifetogether.com/healthplan.

DATE	MY PROGRESS	PARTNER'S PROGRESS

SAMPLE PERSONAL HEALTH PLAN

This worksheet could become your single most important feature in this study. On it you can record your personal priorities before the Father. It will help you live a healthy spiritual life, balancing all five of God's purposes.

PURPOSE	PLAN
CONNECT	WHO are you connecting with spiritually? *Bill and I will meet weekly by email or phone.*
GROW	WHAT is your next step for growth? *Regular devotions or journaling my prayers 2x/week*
DEVELOP	WHERE are you serving? *Serving in Children's Ministry* *Go through GIFTS class*
SHARE	WHEN are you shepherding another in Christ? *Shepherding Bill at lunch or hosting a starter group in the fall*
SURRENDER	HOW are you surrendering your heart? *Help with our teenager* *New job situation*

DATE	MY PROGRESS	PARTNER'S PROGRESS
3/5	Talked during our group	Figured out our goals together
3/12	Missed our time together	Missed our time together
3/26	Met for coffee and review of my goals	Met for coffee
4/10	Emailed prayer requests	Bill sent me his prayer requests
3/5	Great start on personal journaling	Read Mark 1–6 in one sitting!
3/12	Traveled and not doing well this week	Journaled about Christ as Healer
3/26	Back on track	Busy and distracted; asked for prayer
3/1	Need to call Children's Pastor	
3/26	Group did a serving project together	Agreed to lead group worship
3/30	Regularly rotating leadership	Led group worship—great job!
3/5	Called Jim to see if he's open to joining our group	Wanted to invite somebody, but didn't
3/12	Preparing to start a group this fall	
3/30	Group prayed for me	Told friend something he's learning about Christ
3/5	Overwhelmed but encouraged	Scared to lead worship
3/15	Felt heard and more settled	Issue with wife
3/30	Read book on teens	Glad he took on his fear

JOURNALING 101

Henri Nouwen says effective and lasting ministry *for* God grows out of a quiet place alone *with* God. This is why journaling is so important.

The greatest adventure of our lives is found in the daily pursuit of knowing, growing in, serving, sharing, and worshiping Christ forever. This is the essence of a purposeful life: to see all five biblical purposes fully formed and balanced in our lives. Only then are we "complete in Christ" (Colossians 1:28, NASB).

David poured his heart out to God by writing psalms. The book of Psalms contains many of his honest conversations with God in written form, including expressions of every imaginable emotion on every aspect of his life. Like David, we encourage you to select a strategy to integrate God's Word and journaling into your devotional time. Use any of the following resources:

- Bible
- One-year Bible
- New Testament Bible Challenge Reading Plan
  (www.lifetogether.com/readingprograms)
- Devotional book
- Topical Bible study plan

Before or after you read a portion of God's Word, speak to God in honest reflection or response in the form of a written prayer. You may begin this time by simply finishing the sentence "Father . . . ," "Yesterday Lord . . . ," or "Thank you, God, for. . . ." Share with him where you are at the present moment; express your hurts, disappointments, frustrations, blessings, victories, gratefulness. Whatever you do with your journal, make a plan that fits you so you'll have a positive experience. Consider sharing highlights of your progress and experiences with some or all of your group members, especially your spiritual partner(s). You may find they want to join and even encourage you in this journey. Most of all, enjoy the ride and cultivate a more authentic, growing walk with God.

BIBLE READING PLAN

30 Days through the Gospel of Luke

Imagine sitting at the feet of Jesus himself: the Teacher who knows how to live life well, the Savior who died for you, the Lord who commands the universe. Like his first disciples, you can follow him around, watch what he does, listen to what he says, and pattern your life after his.

On the next page is a plan for reading through the gospel of Luke. Luke has a heart for outsiders. Luke himself is a non-Jew who embraced a Jewish Messiah, so he knows what it's like to be an outsider welcomed in. He's fascinated by the way Jesus treats women, the poor, non-Jews, and persons of disreputable character.

Find a quiet place, and have ready a notebook or journal in which you can write what you learn and what you want to say back to God. You may also use the Reflections page at the end of each session of this study. It's helpful to have one or two simple questions in mind to focus your reading. Here are some suggestions:

- What do I *learn* from the life of Christ (his identity, personality, priorities)?
- How does he want me to *live* differently?

  Or,

- How did Jesus treat people?
- How did he turn the normal rules of winners and losers upside down?
- How does he want me to respond to what he said and did?

When we've sat at the Master's feet like this ourselves, the sense of a real, alive, present Jesus has been breathtaking. We pray you'll have the same experience.

☐ Day 1   Luke 1
☐ Day 2   Luke 2
☐ Day 3   Luke 3
☐ Day 4   Luke 4
☐ Day 5   Luke 5
☐ Day 6   Luke 6:1–26
☐ Day 7   Luke 6:27–49
☐ Day 8   Luke 7:1–35
☐ Day 9   Luke 7:36–50
☐ Day 10 Luke 8:1–21
☐ Day 11 Luke 8:22–56
☐ Day 12 Luke 9:1–27
☐ Day 13 Luke 9:28–62
☐ Day 14 Luke 10
☐ Day 15 Luke 11

☐ Day 16 Luke 12:1–21
☐ Day 17 Luke 12:22–59
☐ Day 18 Luke 13
☐ Day 19 Luke 14
☐ Day 20 Luke 15
☐ Day 21 Luke 16
☐ Day 22 Luke 17
☐ Day 23 Luke 18
☐ Day 24 Luke 19
☐ Day 25 Luke 20
☐ Day 26 Luke 21
☐ Day 27 Luke 22:1–38
☐ Day 28 Luke 22:39–71
☐ Day 29 Luke 23
☐ Day 30 Luke 24

LEADING FOR THE FIRST TIME

- **Sweaty palms are a healthy sign.** The Bible says God is gracious to the humble. Remember who is in control; the time to worry is when you're not worried. Those who are soft in heart (and sweaty-palmed) are those whom God is sure to speak through.

- **Seek support.** Ask your leader, coleader, or close friend to pray for you and prepare with you before the session. Walking through the study will help you anticipate potentially difficult questions and discussion topics.

- **Bring your uniqueness to the study.** Lean into who you are and how God wants you to uniquely lead the study.

- **Prepare. Prepare. Prepare.** Go through the session several times. If you are using the DVD, listen to the teaching segment and Leadership Lifter. Go to www.lifetogether.com and download pertinent files. Consider writing in a journal or fasting for a day to prepare yourself for what God wants to do.

- **Don't wait until the last minute to prepare.**

- **Ask for feedback so you can grow.** Perhaps in an email or on cards handed out at the study, have everyone write down three things you did well and one thing you could improve on. Don't get defensive, but show an openness to learn and grow.

- **Use online resources.** Go to www.lifetogether.com and listen to Brett Eastman share the weekly Leadership Lifter and download any additional notes or ideas for your session. You may also want to subscribe to the DOING LIFE TOGETHER Newsletter and LLT Newsletter. Both can be obtained for free by signing up at www.lifetogether.com/subscribe.

- **Prayerfully consider launching a new group.** This doesn't need to happen overnight, but God's heart is for this to happen over time. Not all

Christians are called to be leaders or teachers, but we are all called to be "shepherds" of a few someday.

- **Share with your group what God is doing in your heart.** God is searching for those whose hearts are fully his. Share your trials and victories. We promise that people will relate.

- **Prayerfully consider whom you would like to pass the baton to next week.** It's only fair. God is ready for the next member of your group to go on the faith journey you just traveled. Make it fun, and expect God to do the rest.

HOSTING AN
OPEN HOUSE

If you're starting a new group, try planning an "open house" before your first formal group meeting. Even if you only have two to four core members, it's a great way to break the ice and to consider prayerfully who else might be open to join you over the next few weeks. You can also use this kick-off meeting to hand out study guides, spend some time getting to know each other, discuss each person's expectations for the group, and briefly pray for each other.

A simple meal or good desserts always make a kick-off meeting more fun. After people introduce themselves and share how they ended up being at the meeting (you can play a game to see who has the wildest story!), have everyone respond to a few icebreaker questions: "What is your favorite family vacation?" or "What is one thing you love about your church/our community?" or "What are three things about your life growing up that most people here don't know?" See www.lifetogether.com for more icebreaker ideas.

Next, ask everyone to tell what he or she hopes to get out of the study. You might want to review the LIFE TOGETHER Agreement (pages 80–81) and talk about each person's expectations and priorities.

Finally, set an open chair (maybe two) in the center of your group and explain that it represents someone who would enjoy or benefit from this group but who isn't here yet. Ask people to pray about whom they could invite to join the group over the next few weeks. Hand out postcards (see www.lifetogether.com for examples) and have everyone write an invitation or two. Don't worry about ending up with too many people—you can always have one discussion circle in the living room and another in the dining room after you watch the lesson. Each group could then report prayer requests and progress at the end of the session.

You can skip this kick-off meeting if your time is limited, but you'll experience a huge benefit if you take the time to connect with each other in this way.

EXPERIENCING CHRIST TOGETHER
IN A SUNDAY SCHOOL SETTING

Sunday school is one of the best places to begin building community in your church, and the EXPERIENCING CHRIST TOGETHER DVDs and study guides work in concert to help your Sunday school leadership team do it easily and effectively.

Each study guide of the LIFE TOGETHER curriculum includes a companion DVD with today's top Christian leaders speaking to the passage of Scripture under discussion. Here is one way to use the DVD in a Sunday school class:

- Moderator introduction: welcome the class, and read the Scripture passage for the session
- DVD teaching segment: ten to fifteen minutes
- Small group discussion: divide into small groups of eight to twelve and, using the questions from the curriculum, discuss how the passage applies to each person in the class

So often Sunday school consists of the star teacher with little involvement from others. To use the EXPERIENCING CHRIST TOGETHER DVDs effectively means recruiting a host of people to participate in the Sunday school program. We recommend four teams:

Moderators. These are the facilitators or leaders of the class. Their role is to transition the class through each step in the time together. For example, the moderator will welcome the class and open with prayer. In addition, he or she will introduce the DVD segment by reading the Scripture passage for the session. We recommend that you recruit several moderaters. That allows you to rotate the moderators each week. Doing so takes the pressure off people to commit to every week of the class—and it offers more people opportunity for upfront leadership. One church recruited three sets of moderators (a total of six) because the Sunday school leaders wanted to use the curriculum for twelve weeks. They knew that out of twelve weeks, one set of moderators would, likely, burn out; it's difficult for anyone to provide leadership for twelve straight weeks.

Discussion Guides. These are people who lead the follow-up discussion after the DVD teaching segment. If, for example, your Sunday school runs for an hour, you may want to plan on fifteen to twenty minutes for the DVD teaching segment and an additional twenty to thirty minutes in small group discussion afterward. One church recruited many of its seniors to lead the discussion groups. Some of them had felt excluded from ministry, and the role of discussion guide opened the door for them to serve.

Each discussion guide needs only to read through the passage and the questions in each study guide for preparation. After the DVD teaching segment, the moderator of the class asks the discussion guides to stand up. Then, people circle their chairs around each discussion guide. It's an easy way to create small groups each week. You may need to help some groups find more people or other groups to divide once more, if they end up too large. One church asked some of the discussion guides to move their groups into different rooms, because the seniors had a hard time hearing.

Hospitality Coordinators. These are those who oversee the food and drink for the class. Some classes may not provide this, but for those who do, it's important that multiple people join the team, so one or two people don't burn out over the course of the class.

Technical Coordinators. There's nothing worse than a DVD player that doesn't seem to work. Recruit at least one person to oversee making sure the DVD works each week. It's best, though, to recruit two or three people, in order to rotate them throughout the Sunday school series. It's important that the technical team has made sure the DVD player works *before* the class begins.

One church decided to gather all the adult Sunday school classes together for a twelve-week series using the LIFE TOGETHER DVD and study guides. What happened was amazing—instead of Sunday school starting off with 140 people and ending up with half that many at the end of the fall, attendance stayed high the entire time. Instead of one Sunday school class being led by one or two teachers, more than thirty-five people were involved in some kind of leadership—as moderators, discussion guides, hospitality (food) coordinators, or technical coordinators. The fifteen-minute time at the beginning of Sunday school for coffee and snacks (fruit, coffee cake, etc.) proved just as valuable as the content portion!

The fall program gave the church a new vision for how Sunday school can support the larger issue of spiritual formation and life change. For more ideas and practical tools to strengthen your small group ministry, go to www.lifetogethertoday.com.

INTRODUCTION

If your group is new, or even if you haven't been together for a few weeks, we recommend that you plan a kick-off meeting where you will pray, hand out study guides, spend some time getting to know each other, and discuss each person's expectations for the group. A meeting like this is a great way to start a group or step up people's commitments.

Most groups, if reconvened after a short break, will be renewed in seeing each other and open to increasing their commitment as much as 25 percent. We have seen some naturally move to a weekly format, begin doing homework, and commit to daily devotions simply because the leader shared his or her heart. What do you sense God wants from you and your group?

However, if your group is brand new, a simple meal, potluck, or even good desserts make a kick-off meeting more fun. After dessert, have everyone respond to an icebreaker question, such as, "How did you hear of this church, and what's one thing you love about it?" Or, "Tell us three things about your life growing up that most people here don't know."

Then ask everyone to tell what he or she hopes to get out of this study. You might want to review the LIFE TOGETHER Agreement (see pages 80–81 and talk about each person's expectations and priorities. You could discuss whether you want to do Bible study homework before each meeting—homework covering the questions under the Growing and/or the For Deeper Study sections. Review the Small Group Calendar on page 82 and talk about who else is willing to open their home or facilitate a meeting.

Finally, cast the vision, as Jesus did, to be inclusive not exclusive. Ask everyone to think of people who would enjoy or benefit from a group like this. The beginning of a new study is a great time to welcome a few people into your circle. Have each person share a name or two and either make phone calls the coming week or handwrite invitations or postcards that very night. This will make it fun and also make it happen. At www.lifetogether .com we have a free email invitation you may send to every potential member. Don't worry about ending up with too many people—you can always have one discussion circle in the living room and another in the dining room.

SESSION ONE:
AS I HAVE LOVED YOU

As a leader, your most important job is to create an atmosphere where people are willing to talk honestly about what Christ's words and actions have to do with them. Especially if your group is new, be available before people arrive so you can greet them at the door. People are naturally nervous at a new group, so a hug or handshake can help put them at ease.

If your group is new and you aren't able to hold a kick-off meeting before you launch into session 1, consider starting this first meeting half an hour early to give people time to socialize without shortchanging your study time. For example, you can have social time from 7:00 to 7:30, and by 7:40 you'll gather the group with a prayer. Even if only a few people are seated in the living room by 7:40, ask them to join you in praying for those who are coming and for God to be present among you as you meet. Others will notice you praying and will sit down.

Question 1. We've designed this study for both seekers and believers. Believers may want to talk about God's love, but this question includes an option for those who would prefer to talk about human love. You should be the first to answer this question while others are thinking about how to respond. Be sure to give everyone a chance to respond to this question, because it's a chance for the group to get to know each other. It's not necessary to go around the circle in order.

Introduction to the Series. If this is your first LIFE TOGETHER study, take a moment after question 1 to orient the group to one principle that undergirds this series: *A healthy small group balances the purposes of the church*. Most small groups emphasize Bible study, fellowship, and prayer. But God has called us to reach out to others as well. He wants us to *do* what Jesus teaches, not just *learn about* it. You may spend less time in this series studying the Bible than some group members are used to. That's because you'll spend more time doing things the Bible says believers should do.

However, those who like more Bible study can find plenty of it in this series. If your group likes to do deeper Bible study, consider having members answer next week's Growing section questions ahead of time as homework. They can even study next week's For Deeper Study passages for homework too. Then, during the Growing portion of your meeting, you can share the high points of what you've learned.

If the five biblical purposes are new to your group, be sure to review them together on pages 8–10 of the Read Me First section.

Question 2. An agreement helps you clarify your group's priorities and cast new vision for what the group can be. Members can imagine what your group could be like if they lived these values. So turn to pages 80–81 and choose one value that you want to emphasize in this study. We've suggested some options. If you choose "rotating leaders," you don't need to invest a lot of time in it now. In session 3 you'll have a chance to plan who will lead each meeting.

Question 3. Have someone read the Bible passage aloud. It's a good idea to ask someone ahead of time, because not everyone is comfortable reading aloud in public. When the passage has been read, ask question 3. *It is not necessary that everyone answer every question in the Bible study.* In fact, a group can become boring if you simply go around the circle and give answers. Your goal is to create a discussion—which means that perhaps only a few people respond to each question and an engaging dialogue gets going.

Jesus repeats several interrelated instructions: Remain in my love. Remain in my love by obeying my commands. Obey my command to love one another. Thus, remaining (abiding, dwelling) in Jesus' love can't be separated from loving one another.

Question 5. Some possibilities are sacrificial, costly, committed, practical, and generous.

Question 6. In verses 9–10, Jesus says that obeying his commands helps us dwell in his love. Verse 12 makes clear that his command to love is primary. So the more we love others, the more we rest and dwell in Christ's love for us. And the more aware we are of Christ's love for us, the more our love for others should naturally follow.

Question 8. Love involves noticing people's needs and responding to them. It is intensely practical.

Question 12. We've offered several options for personal time with God. Don't press seekers to do this, but every believer should have a plan for personal time with God. There's a Reflections page at the end of every session of this study for them to write down what they discover.

Those who prefer topical Bible study might want to answer the For Deeper Study questions each week. If your group is accustomed to doing Bible study homework before each meeting, this is a great choice.

For those who have done a lot of Bible study, we encourage the meditation option. Living with one short passage each week can help them move biblical truth from their heads into their hearts and actions.

It's perfectly fine if one person chooses one option and someone else chooses another. One principle of life together is to champion each other's dreams and goals.

Question 13. The "Circles of Life" diagram is a vivid symbol of one of the values of the LIFE TOGETHER Agreement: "welcome for newcomers." Some groups fear that newcomers will interrupt the intimacy that members have built over time. However, groups generally gain strength with the infusion of new blood. It's like a river of living water flowing into a stagnant pond. Some groups remain permanently open, while others open periodically, such as at the beginning and ending of a study. Love grows by giving itself away. If your circle becomes too large for easy face-to-face conversations, you can simply form a second discussion circle in another room in your home.

Give everyone a few moments in which to write down names before each shares. You might pray for these names later in the session. Encourage people not to be afraid to ask someone. Almost no one is annoyed to be invited to something! Most people are honored to be asked, even if they can't make it.

We encourage an outward focus for your group because groups that become too inwardly focused tend to become unhealthy over time. People naturally gravitate to feeding themselves through Bible study, prayer, and social time, so it's usually up to the leader to push them to consider how this inward nourishment can overflow into outward concern for others.

Question 14. Never pressure a person to pray aloud. That's a sure way to scare someone away from your group. Instead of praying in a circle (which makes it obvious when someone stays silent), allow open time when anyone can pray who wishes to do so. Have someone write down everyone's prayer requests on the Prayer and Praise Report (page 21). If your time is short, consider having people share requests and pray with just one or two other people.

SESSION TWO:
SHOWING UP

The Bible teaches that where two or more are gathered together, God is already in their midst. You don't need to wait until everyone has gathered before opening in prayer. Reward those who are on time by starting your meeting on schedule. When several people have arrived, take a few minutes to pray for those on their way and for your time together.

Question 1. This is a great opportunity to get to know each other better, but you will have to manage the time. One way is to appoint someone as timekeeper who will let the group know when each person's one minute is up. That may seem too brief, but people can learn a lot in one minute. If you have ten people and everyone takes two minutes, this question will take twenty minutes, and that's a lot of the group's time. An alternative is to let just two or three people respond to this question. If anyone shares a significant loss that is recent or unresolved, remember this for your prayer time. Or pause right there and pray briefly for the person.

Question 2. Again, don't let everyone respond to all of the Bible study questions. You want a discussion, not just going around the circle and sharing. Two or three responses to this question will be enough.

Question 3. People will see different things. For example, Martha is remarkably frank, especially as a woman in that culture addressing a rabbi. She lets him know she's disappointed, and she doesn't hesitate to ask Jesus to perform a miracle even now. Jesus focuses on encouraging her faith in who he is and what he can do. Martha is a think-and-act kind of person, and Jesus relates to her on that level.

Question 4. While Martha runs to meet Jesus, Mary waits until Jesus asks for her. Her grief comes out in strong and tender emotions, such as falling at his feet and weeping. Jesus is tender to her in return. Her tears draw out his tears, although she weeps in grief and he weeps more in anger at death and the unbelief of Mary's friends. The point of these questions is to see how Jesus responds to his friends differently, according to their needs and temperaments. There's no one-size-fits-all response to someone in grief. Jesus brings thought, emotion, and action to the situation.

Question 6. It's important never to use Bible verses as pat answers to someone in grief. Mary and Martha knew the doctrine of resurrection in the future; what they needed was someone to respond to them in the now. The doctrine is crucial, but we need to bring it to people with our emotion and action fully engaged.

Question 7. Showing up for his friends set Jesus up for death. We won't often be called upon to sacrifice that much, but it's our model. We need to be prepared to pay the costs of love.

Question 10. For those who haven't done a LIFE TOGETHER study before, spiritual partners will be a new idea. We highly encourage you to try pairs or triplets for one month. It's so hard to sustain a spiritual practice like prayer or consistent Bible reading with no support. A friend makes a huge difference. Partners can check in with each other weekly either at the beginning of your group meetings or outside the meeting.

Questions 11 and 12. Try to save plenty of time for prayer, as a discussion of loss may have raised group members' needs to the surface. You can't raise the dead, but you can follow Jesus' example of being totally present. And you can pray to the One who can raise the dead and heal all losses.

Questions 1 and 2. We strongly encourage you to give spiritual partners a try (question 2). You can let partners connect in every other session if it's hard to do it each week. But if you plan the partner's check-in time during your meeting for a few weeks, you may find that people love doing it and even begin to schedule check-in times outside the meetings.

Question 5. Jesus did tell the woman to leave her life of sin (John 8:11). He didn't condone adultery; he simply saw a more redemptive way of dealing with it than the death penalty.

Question 7. Most people have a harder time dealing with someone whose sin is sexual than with someone with other sins. Sexual sins trigger us. But in God's eyes, they're not worse. If someone's sin is harming others, then a community needs to decide how to care for the sinner and those sinned against. The goal is to seek everyone's best interest. The best interest of the sinner is usually to stay within the community while taking steps to overcome the sin. This often requires a combination of loving confrontation, accountability, and support. It's often a messy process, as well as costly for those who engage in it.

Question 9. Loving sinners without condoning sin requires us to grow inside. The more aware we are of our own sin, and of how much God has forgiven us, the more we will naturally respond to other sinners with love and wisdom. The more we tell ourselves that we're "fine" and other people are the sinners, the less able we'll be to do what Jesus did. If we are engaged in a process of overcoming our own sin, we'll have the resources to help others do the same.

Question 11. As leader, you are in the people development business. Your job is to help group members grow into disciples and ministers over time. In order to discover and develop their unique gifts, they need opportunities to experiment with service. You may not need their help (in fact, it may be more work to coach them), but they need to share the load in the group. Don't be shocked if people don't volunteer to take on these roles. You may need to go up to them during social time after the meeting and ask them to take on something that you think will fit them. Your personal invitation and affirmation of their abilities will make a huge difference to them.

SESSION FOUR:
TRUTHFUL BUT TENDER

Question 3. You can deal with this question briefly with just one or two responses. The point here is that Jesus was generous with praise. That's an important backdrop for understanding his strong criticism of Peter later in the passage.

Question 6. Many of us would feel devastated if our mentor said this to us. These are strong words, and if Jesus is our model for relationships, we need to deal forthrightly with what we see on the page.

Question 8. Jesus did not rebuke Peter because he felt offended. Jesus wasn't motivated by self-importance or a need for everyone to agree with him. He didn't make a habit of criticizing everything his disciples did. This is what sets his rebuke apart from much of the confrontation we see among people around us. What was at stake here was a mission that would decide the fate of humankind. Peter was challenging what Jesus knew was the Father's will. He was tempting Jesus to commit a sin. That made this situation so unique that it required strong words.

Question 10. It's essential that we get our pride—our belief that we are better than the other person, that we know what's right about everything, and that we are sinless—out of the way before we confront someone. Strong words from a humble person can bring repentance and healing. Strong words from an arrogant, judgmental person simply wound.

Question 14. You may want to have the various circles move to different rooms of the home for this role-playing exercise. If you've never done this kind of thing, take a risk. People usually enjoy role-playing, and they learn a great deal.

SESSION FIVE:
EXTREME FORGIVENESS

Because the passage you're discussing in this session is so often misunderstood, it will be helpful for you to read the Study Notes ahead of time and be prepared to direct that information to the group at appropriate times.

Question 3. The obvious response is that most of us have trouble living by most of these commands. You might want to set an example of honesty in answering this question.

Question 4. This is a key question. Jesus wants us to relate to others in this startling way because (1) that's how God acts, (2) imitating God shows that we are truly his children, (3) some kind of reward awaits those who live in this costly way, and (4) if we don't live in this merciful, generous way, we can expect to be treated without mercy and generosity. We will never develop the habits Jesus teaches until we deeply grasp that we have been God's enemies, and he has loved us. We have taken what belongs to God, and he has given us even more than we have stolen. We need to be gripped by God's mercy toward us, and we need to see ourselves and others through his eyes.

Before you discuss this question, it will be helpful to read the Study Notes. Jesus' commands are often misunderstood.

Questions 11, 12, and 13. If you prefer, you may go straight from the Bible study to question 14 (prayer) and then return to these questions after about fifteen minutes. You'll need to watch the clock during prayer time so you don't run out of time for these outward-looking questions. Most groups will spend all their time on Bible study and prayer (nurturing themselves) if the leader doesn't deliberately move them to think about outreach. Outreach doesn't come naturally, but it's invaluable for sparking growth in individuals.

We've offered a couple of options for outreach. One is a service project. In order to develop others' gifts, we urge you to tap a couple of group members to plan this project. You may need to give them personal invitations if they're reluctant to volunteer.

The other option may seem radical: taking six weeks off from your group to help one or more other groups get started. You'll need to plant the vision in members' hearts: Jesus' dream is for every sheep to find a shepherd, and for every member to help him shepherd a few people. Ask your pastor how your group can help launch new groups.

Question 14. This could be a tender time. Most of us have people in our lives whom we have trouble forgiving. We also have sins for which we need forgiveness. Before group members get into smaller circles, remind them that nothing said in their circles may be repeated outside the circle. Confidentiality is essential. Some people will be more reluctant to confess anything deeply personal, and that's okay. This is a chance for people to connect at whatever level of trust they've developed so far.

Question 15. If your time is short, you might recruit some people after the meeting to plan worship for your final session in this study. Depending on how your church handles Communion, consider planning a time when your group can celebrate the Lord's Supper within the group or together at your church.

SESSION SIX:
CROSS-SHAPED LOVE

Questions 1 and 2. As always, you have the option to let the whole group reflect on their week (question 1) or to let partners support each other in their personal walks with God.

Question 5. Read all four of these passages ahead of time to see which ones you think would be most helpful. You can even recruit another group member to research what Jesus' death accomplished and bring that information to the group. He or she can read the passages listed under For Deeper Study, examine the Study Notes, and perhaps consult a commentary or someone on your church staff. It's surprising how many believers have only the vaguest notion of what Jesus' death did for them. But the more we are gripped by this act of love, the more natural it will be for us to love others in costly ways. That's the point of this discussion: not an academic understanding of the cross, but an understanding that motivates group members to love the way Christ has loved them.

Questions 8, 9, and 10. These questions aim to reach people's hearts. It's not enough to intellectually understand the crucifixion and what scholars call "the atonement." We need to be horrified by our own sin and therefore be profoundly grateful for God's forgiveness. Some believers fail to grow in love because they still feel ashamed of their sin and don't truly grasp that they've been completely forgiven. Others fail to grow in love because they don't want to look closely at their lives to see all the sin that has needed forgiveness. Help your group understand *both* their sin *and* God's forgiveness. You could set a great example by telling the group about a recent situation when you failed to love someone as you should, and how God's forgiveness affects you now.

Question 12. The next natural step in this series would be either *Growing in Christ Together* or *Sharing Christ Together*. If your group tends to emphasize inner growth over outward service, *Sharing Christ Together* might help them gain balance. *Serving Like Christ Together* is another outwardly focused option.

Question 13. If anyone in your group is going out temporarily to serve another group, be sure to give him or her a tremendous demonstration of your support.

ABOUT THE AUTHORS

The authors' previous work as a team includes the DOING LIFE TOGETHER Bible study series, which won a Silver Medallion from the Evangelical Christian Publishers Association, as well as the DOING LIFE TOGETHER DVD series.

Brett Eastman has served as the champion of Small Groups and Leadership Development for both Willow Creek Community Church and Saddleback Valley Community Church. Brett is now the Founder and CEO of Lifetogether, a ministry whose mission is to "transform lives through community." Brett earned his Masters of Divinity degree from Talbot School of Theology and his Management Certificate from Kellogg School of Business at Northwestern University. **Dee Eastman** is the real hero in the family, who, after giving birth to Joshua and Breanna, gave birth to identical triplets—Meagan, Melody, and Michelle. They live in Las Flores, California.

Todd and Denise Wendorff serve at King's Harbor Church in Redondo Beach, California. Todd is a teaching pastor, handles leadership development, and pastors men. He is also coauthor of the Every Man Bible Study Series. Denise speaks to women at conferences, classes, and special events. She also serves women through personal discipleship. Previously, Todd was on the pastoral staff at Harvest Bible Chapel, Willow Creek Community Church, and Saddleback Valley Community Church. He holds a Th.M. from Talbot School of Theology. Todd and Denise live in Rolling Hills Estates, California with their three children, Brooke, Brittany, and Brandon.

Karen Lee-Thorp has written or cowritten more than fifty books and Bible studies, including *How to Ask Great Questions* and *Why Beauty Matters*. Her previous Silver Medallion winners are *The Story of Stories*, *LifeChange: Ephesians*, and *LifeChange: Revelation*. She was a senior editor at NavPress for many years and series editor for the LifeChange Bible study series. She is now a freelance writer, speaks at women's retreats, and trains small group leaders. She lives in Brea, California, with her husband, Greg Herr, and their daughters, Megan and Marissa.

SMALL GROUP ROSTER

Name	Address	Phone	Email Address	Team or Role	Church Ministry
Bill Jones	7 Almalar Street L.F. 92665	766-2255	bjones@aol.com	Socials	children's ministry

(Pass your book around your group at your first meeting to get everyone's name and contact information.)

Name	Address	Phone	Email Address	Team or Role	Church Ministry

Experiencing Christ Together:
Living with Purpose in Community
Brett & Dee Eastman; Todd & Denise Wendorff;
Karen Lee-Thorp

Experiencing Christ Together: Living with Purpose in Community is a series of six, six-week study guides that offers small groups a chance to explore Jesus' teaching on the five biblical purposes of the church. By closely examining Christ's life and teaching in the Gospels, the series helps group members walk in the steps of Christ's early followers. Jesus lived every moment following God's purposes for his life, and Experiencing Christ Together helps groups learn how they can do this too. The first book lays the foundation: who Christ is and what he has done for us. Each of the other five books in the series looks at how Jesus trained his followers to live one of the five biblical purposes (fellowship, disciple-ship, service, evangelism, and worship).

	Softcovers	DVD
Beginning in Christ Together	ISBN: 0-310-24986-4	ISBN: 0-310-26187-2
Connecting in Christ Together	ISBN: 0-310-24981-3	ISBN: 0-310-26189-9
Growing in Christ Together	ISBN: 0-310-24985-6	ISBN: 0-310-26192-9
Serving Like Christ Together	ISBN: 0-310-24984-8	ISBN: 0-310-26194-5
Sharing Christ Together	ISBN: 0-310-24983-X	ISBN: 0-310-26196-1
Surrendering to Christ Together	ISBN: 0-310-24982-1	ISBN: 0-310-26198-8

Pick up a copy today at your favorite bookstore!

ZONDERVAN™

GRAND RAPIDS, MICHIGAN 49530 USA

WWW.ZONDERVAN.COM

life**together**.com

Beginning in Christ Together
Brett & Dee Eastman; Todd &
Denise Wendorff; Karen Lee-Thorp

Beginning in Christ Together allows you to get to
know Jesus as his first followers did. They met
him as Teacher, a rabbi. They came to know him
as Healer, Shepherd, Servant, Savior, and ultimately Risen Lord. From his first words, "follow
me," through his ministry, death, and resurrection, he kept drawing them deeper into his life.

Experiencing Christ Together: Living with Purpose in Community is
a series of six, six-week study guides that offers small groups a chance to
explore Jesus' teaching on the five biblical purposes of the church.
Beginning in Christ Together, the first book, lays the foundation: who
Christ is and what he has done for us. Each of the other five books in the
series looks at how Jesus trained his followers to live one of the five biblical purposes (fellowship, discipleship, service, evangelism, and worship).

Softcover: 0-310-24986-4
DVD: 0-310-26187-2

Pick up a copy today at your favorite bookstore!

ZONDERVAN™

GRAND RAPIDS, MICHIGAN 49530 USA

WWW.ZONDERVAN.COM

Connecting in Christ Together

Brett & Dee Eastman; Todd &
Denise Wendorff; Karen Lee-Thorp

Today, love is not always the first thing that springs to mind when unbelievers think about Christians. But it should be. Our mandate from Jesus is simple: "Love one another as I have loved you." What Christians call "fellowship" is one of God's core dreams for his people. It's simply love, passionate and practical. If you need more of that in your life and your group, study *Connecting in Christ Together* and let Jesus show you how.

Experiencing Christ Together: Living with Purpose in Community is a series of six, six-week study guides that offers small groups a chance to explore Jesus' teaching on the five biblical purposes of the church. The first book lays the foundation: who Christ is and what he has done for us. Each of the other five books in the series, including this one, looks at how Jesus trained his followers to live one of the five biblical purposes (fellowship, discipleship, service, evangelism, and worship).

Softcover: 0-310-24981-3
DVD: 0-310-26189-9

Pick up a copy today at your favorite bookstore!

GRAND RAPIDS, MICHIGAN 49530 USA
WWW.ZONDERVAN.COM

Growing in Christ Together

*Brett & Dee Eastman; Todd &
Denise Wendorff; Karen Lee-Thorp*

Jesus was the most remarkable rabbi of his day.
He is also the most remarkable rabbi of our day,
for he's still alive. If we're willing to be his followers, we can learn to do life the way Jesus
would if he had our temperaments, our families,
and our jobs. *Growing in Christ Together* can
help us to get our priorities in order.

Experiencing Christ Together: Living with Purpose in Community is
a series of six, six-week study guides that offers small groups a chance
to explore Jesus' teaching on the five biblical purposes of the church.
The first book lays the foundation: who Christ is and what he has done
for us. Each of the other five books in the series, including this one, looks
at how Jesus trained his followers to live one of the five biblical purposes (fellowship, discipleship, service, evangelism, and worship).

Softcover: 0-310-24985-6
DVD: 0-310-26192-9

Pick up a copy today at your favorite bookstore!

ZONDERVAN™

GRAND RAPIDS, MICHIGAN 49530 USA

WWW.ZONDERVAN.COM

life**together**.com

Serving Like Christ Together

Brett & Dee Eastman; Todd &
Denise Wendorff; Karen Lee-Thorp

Serviced shouldn't be something we force ourselves to do because we'll be punished if we
don't. It should flow from a heart formed as
Christ's is, by a passion for something greater
than ourselves. *Serving Like Christ Together*
investigates six qualities of a servant's heart that
Jesus highly valued.

Experiencing Christ Together: Living with Purpose in Community is
a series of six, six-week study guides that offers small groups a chance
to explore Jesus' teaching on the five biblical purposes of the church.
The first book lays the foundation: who Christ is and what he has done
for us. Each of the other five books in the series, including this one, looks
at how Jesus trained his followers to live one of the five biblical purposes (fellowship, discipleship, service, evangelism, and worship).

Softcover: 0-310-24984-8
DVD: 0-310-26194-5

Pick up a copy today at your favorite bookstore!

ZONDERVAN™

GRAND RAPIDS, MICHIGAN 49530 USA
WWW.ZONDERVAN.COM

life**together**.com

Sharing Christ Together
Brett & Dee Eastman; Todd &
Denise Wendorff; Karen Lee-Thorp

Jesus asks us to do what he did: help lost people learn how to navigate through life and find their Home. It doesn't matter than our map-reading skills aren't perfect yet. As long as we know a little more than someone else, we can gently and respectfully offer help. *Sharing Christ Together* will help you to do three things: develop your compassion for lost people, learn some useful sharing skills, and team up with a group to build relationships among the lost.

Experiencing Christ Together: Living with Purpose in Community is a series of six, six-week study guides that offers small groups a chance to explore Jesus' teaching on the five biblical purposes of the church. The first book lays the foundation: who Christ is and what he has done for us. Each of the other five books in the series, including this one, looks at how Jesus trained his followers to live one of the five biblical purposes (fellowship, discipleship, service, evangelism, and worship).

Softcover: 0-310-24983-X
DVD: 0-310-26196-1

Pick up a copy today at your favorite bookstore!

GRAND RAPIDS, MICHIGAN 49530 USA
WWW.ZONDERVAN.COM

Surrendering to Christ Together

*Brett & Dee Eastman; Todd &
Denise Wendorff; Karen Lee-Thorp*

In *Surrendering to Christ Together*, you'll investigate six heart attitudes that can motivate you
to totally abandon yourself to God's agenda. If
you've been holding back something from God
for fear of failure or loss, or because you're too busy pursuing your own
goals, take a good look at what motivated Jesus and his closest friends.

Experiencing Christ Together: Living with Purpose in Community is
a series of six, six-week study guides that offers small groups a chance
to explore Jesus' teaching on the five biblical purposes of the church.
The first book lays the foundation: who Christ is and what he has done
for us. Each of the other five books in the series, including this one, looks
at how Jesus trained his followers to live one of the five biblical purposes (fellowship, discipleship, service, evangelism, and worship).

Softcover: 0-310-24982-1
DVD: 0-310-26198-8

Pick up a copy today at your favorite bookstore!

GRAND RAPIDS, MICHIGAN 49530 USA

WWW.ZONDERVAN.COM

Doing Life Together series

Brett & Dee Eastman; Todd & Denise Wendorff;
Karen Lee-Thorp

Based on the five biblical purposes that form the bedrock of Saddleback Church, Doing Life Together will help your group discover what God created you for and how you can turn this dream into an everyday reality. Experience the transformation firsthand as you begin Connecting, Growing, Developing, Sharing, and Surrendering your life together for him.

"Doing Life Together is a groundbreaking study . . . [It's] the first small group curriculum built completely on the purpose-driven paradigm . . . The greatest reason I'm excited about [it] is that I've seen the dramatic changes it produces in the lives of those who study it."
—FROM THE FOREWORD BY RICK WARREN

Small Group Ministry Consultation

Building a healthy, vibrant, and growing small group ministry is challenging. That's why Brett Eastman and a team of certified coaches are offering small group ministry consultation. Join pastors and church leaders from around the country to discover new ways to launch and lead a healthy Purpose-Driven small group ministry in your church. To find out more information please call 1-800-467-1977.

	Softcover
Beginning Life Together	ISBN: 0-310-24672-5
Connecting with God's Family	ISBN: 0-310-24673-3
Growing to Be Like Christ	ISBN: 0-310-24674-1
Developing Your SHAPE to Serve Others	ISBN: 0-310-24675-X
Sharing Your Life Mission Every Day	ISBN: 0-310-24676-8
Surrendering Your Life for God's Pleasure	ISBN: 0-310-24677-6
Curriculum Kit	ISBN: 0-310-25002-1

ZONDERVAN™

GRAND RAPIDS, MICHIGAN 49530 USA

WWW.ZONDERVAN.COM

life**together**.com

Doing Life Together DVD series

Brett & Dee Eastman; Todd & Denise Wendorff;
Karen Lee-Thorp

The Doing Life Together series on DVD provides small group members with basic training on how to live healthy and balanced lives—purpose driven lives. Each DVD features practical techniques for leading small groups; a personal story, interview, drama, or music video related to the weekly topic; dynamic teaching featuring well-known teachers such as Bruce Wilkinson, John Ortberg, Carol Kent, Joe Stowell, and Erwin McManus; and worship music featuring the songs of Maranatha!

Based on the five biblical purposes that form the bedrock of Saddleback Church, Doing Life Together is a comprehensive study of the Purpose-Driven® Life. It will help you cultivate a healthy, balanced Christian life together with a friend, small group, or even your entire church. This experienced team of writers will take you on a spiritual journey, discovering not only what God created you for but also how you can turn that dream into an everyday reality. Experience the transformation firsthand as you Begin, Connect, Grow, Develop, Share, and Surrender your life together for him.

DVDs
Beginning Life Together   ISBN: 0-310-25004-8
Connecting with God's Family   ISBN: 0-310-25005-6
Growing to Be Like Christ   ISBN: 0-310-25006-4
Developing Your SHAPE to Serve Others   ISBN: 0-310-25007-2
Sharing Your Life Mission Every Day   ISBN: 0-310-25008-0
Surrendering Your Life for God's Pleasure   ISBN: 0-310-25009-9

Also available:
Boxed kit of 6 books and 6 DVDs   ISBN: 0-310-25002-1

Pick up a copy today at your favorite bookstore!

ZONDERVAN™

GRAND RAPIDS, MICHIGAN 49530 USA

WWW.ZONDERVAN.COM

life**together**.com

Life Together Student Edition
Brett Eastman & Doug Fields

The Life Together series is the beginning of a relational journey, from being a member of a group to being a vital part of an unbelievable spiritual community. These books will help you think, talk, dig deep, care, heal, share . . . and have the time of your life! Life . . . together!

The Life Together Student Edition DVD Curriculum combines DVD teaching from well-known youth Bible teachers, as well as leadership training, with the Life Together Student Edition Small Group Series to give a new way to do small group study and ministry with basic training on how to live healthy and balanced lives-purpose driven lives.

Thirty-six sessions are included in the six-book curriculum:

STARTING to Go Where God Wants You to Be: 6 Small Group Sessions on Beginning

CONNECTING Your Hearts to Others: 6 Small Group Sessions on Fellowship

GROWING to Be Like Jesus: 6 Small Group Sessions on Discipleship

SERVING Others in Love: 6 Small Group Sessions on Ministry

SHARING Your Story and God's Story: 6 Small Group Sessions on Evangelism

SURRENDERING Your Life to Honor God: 6 Small Group Sessions on Worship

Teaching about the session's core Bible passage and theme, the lesson material takes the burden of correct interpretation off the leader, so less experienced leaders can be confident that their groups' direction stays biblically sound.

The kit includes 6 guides and 3 DVDs with inserts for leaders. Also available are the 6 student editions of the Doing Life Together Bible studies.

0-310-25339-X

 0-310-25340-3

0-310-25341-1

 0-310-25332-2

0-310-25333-0

0-310-25334-9

0-310-25335-7

0-310-25336-5

0-310-25337-3

0-310-25338-1

We want to hear from you. Please send your comments about this book to us in care of zreview@zondervan.com. Thank you.

GRAND RAPIDS, MICHIGAN 49530 USA

WWW.ZONDERVAN.COM